hit me with music

How to Start, Manage, Record, and Perform With Your Own Rock Band

STEPHANIE POWELL

The Millbrook Press
Brookfield, Connecticut

This book, like a band, has been a collective endeavor. I'd like to thank the following people:

Frank Campbell, East Side Flash, Rob Fedson, and Mac MacDonnell for their contributions to the technical chapters • Jane Gillman and Craig Calvert for their insights on life without a day job • American Federation of Musicians, Local 433, and Waterloo Records for general information; Texas Music Association for their "Music 101" series • Amanda Nevitt for her contribution to the section on hearing loss • Frank Menchaca and Kate Nunn for their indispensable contributions as editors • Sophie and Nate Powell for being understanding about countless hours spent at the computer instead of playing Candyland • Doug Powell, whose computer assistance, home-cooked dinners, and loving support made this book possible.

I would also like to extend my appreciation to all the bands I have played in, both past and present. These bands served as the training ground from which most of this text was gleaned; for the fun and good music, I thank you.   S.P.

Diagrams by Sharon Lane Holm

Library of Congress Cataloging-in-Publilcation Data

Powell, Stephanie.
Hit me with music: how to start, manage, record, and perform with your own rock band \ Stephanie Powell.
p. cm.
Includes bibliographical references and index.
ISBN 1-56294-653-6
1. Rock music--Vocational guidance. I.Title.
ML3795.P68 1995
781.66'023--dc20   95-1965   CIP AC MN
Summary: This book guides readers through every aspect of forming and playing in a rock band, from determining style and instrumentation to playing live and recording.

Published by The Millbrook Press
2 Old New Milford Road
Brookfield, Connecticut 06804

Contents

hit me with music

foreword

It's about a dream.
It's about the team.
Find the players.
Sculpt the vision.
Support each other.
Find a style.

Make a statement.
Keep a focus.
Practice hard.
Don't stop trusting.
Make it real.
Get a deal.

Find some magic.
Keep connected.
Play out often.
Never soften.
Build a fan-base.
They will make you.
Don't neglect them.
They can break you.

Keep it clean.
And keep it fresh.
Never lose faith.
Get some rest.
Find a look.
Read this book.

When you're writing, let it flow.
When you need to, let it go.
Keep it honest.
Avoid isolation.
It's a journey,
Not a destination.

When they write reviews
Try not to read them.
If you can't avoid it,
Don't believe them.
Work hard.
Enjoy the process.
Watch for the pitfalls.
It's no bed of roses.

(And always keep
your publishing!)

steven tyler

introduction

Hit Me With Music

One good thing about music
When it hits, you feel no pain
So hit me with music
Hit me with music
     Bob Marley
     "Trenchtown Rock"[1]

Rock hits you.

Maybe you listen to Metallica and Guns 'n' Roses. Or possibly Pearl Jam and Nirvana. The Grateful Dead. Led Zeppelin.

Whatever the band, one thing is certain: The music has an impact on how you think and feel, and that impact is like nothing else. That's why you save up money for your favorite band's next tour, their latest disc, or to buy that earlier one still missing from your collection. One way or another you get the music because it hits you.

And sometimes you wonder if it might do more. What would it be like to be in a band? You know a few chords. No one has to nag you to practice. You enjoy poring over music books and learning licks from discs of your favorite musicians. Maybe you've got ideas for a song or two. Or maybe you and a friend get together to cut up on some tunes, and you're thinking: We should start a band.

Why not? A band is a great way to be with people who love music as much as you do. A band allows you the creative control to play the kind of music you want in the way you want to play it. And who knows? Maybe the music you make will hit someone else.

But before you plug in and let it wail, there are many things to know about being in a band. That is what this book is all about. *Hit Me With Music* covers the highs and lows of life in a band, from choosing a name to booking gigs to recording and much more.

Why do some bands flame out after only a short time, while others, like the Rolling Stones or Aerosmith, still burn up stages after more than twenty years? The answer lies in the fact that a band is not *just* about music. It's also about egos, compromise, and, yes, plain old hard work. But few things are sweeter than a group of musicians coming together and creating a sound that takes both player and listener to music heaven.

Throughout this book, you'll hear from some of the best-known and most respected figures in music, both the young hell-raisers and Rock and Roll Hall of Famers. And though this book focuses on how to start a rock band, most of the information can be applied to almost any kind of band.

chapter one

Join Together: Finding Players

> *I want you to join together with the band.*
> Pete Townshend,
> The Who, "Join Together"[1]

Getting players together is at the core of launching any band. But before you start plastering local music stores with "musician wanted" signs, decide what kind of music you want to play. To the uninformed, rock is a single style. As any serious musician or fan will tell you—and as you probably already know—it is many: metal, grunge, pop, reggae, punk, and others. Many bands combine a number of styles. The Red Hot Chili Peppers, for example, fused metal, pop, and funk into their fierce, rhythmic sound.

It would be impossible—and foolish—to map all the sonic roads available to you as you start a band. Those roads divide and converge so often that any map of them would end up looking like a tangle of recording tape. The best advice is probably the simplest: Choose the style you like the most—regardless of whether you think it is the one most likely to succeed—and be open to influences as you develop. If you're not clear in your own mind what kind of music you want to play, you'll have a tough time convincing others to join your rock and roll crusade.

Style

Whether you are a cover (playing other people's songs), original, or somewhere-in-between band, find a sound that in some way separates you from the multitude of bands in Musicland. A style is the common thread that weaves through your entire repertoire, making the music unmistakably your own. Individual songs may vary, yet that certain quality is always there. Finding a style is no easy task. It takes time for a band's musical stew to simmer, letting the unique flavors emerge. Too often the stress of trying to force a style sours the music and ultimately the band itself. In truth, style is not so much found as discovered.

Having the courage to stay with a style gives a band a sense of identity. Groups that jump from rock to jazz to rhythm and blues to please as many folks as possible come across as insecure. Know the difference between incorporating different sounds in your style and style-hopping to people-please. Ultimately, you've hit the mark when you as a band musically please yourselves. Whether anyone else likes your sound is up to the music gods, and a look at popular music of the last half-century will tell you those gods can be fickle.

Hacking Around

many bands start out with young musicians playing tunes for fun, calling their loose configuration a band. Whether those players go beyond the more relaxed approach is up to the group; the hack-around band is as viable as the band that focuses more intently on rehearsal, performance, and promotion. The key point is that you make your band what you want it to be. Don't force your group to be more than it is. For some new bands, being able to start, play, and end a song all at the same time is a big accomplishment. By the same token, if you want to take your band beyond the garage stage, know that you can only do so with determination, effort, confidence, and planning.

Instrumentation

knowing what kind of music you want to play will help to determine what instruments you'll need and, naturally, what players to look for. Many bands begin with whomever is immediately ready, willing, and (sometimes, though not always) able to play. This accounts for the long tradition of family-based acts ranging from the Jackson Five to Heart to the All-man Brothers.

Instrumentation is the bedrock of your band's sound. A band's sound takes time to emerge and will change over time. That sound can be unlike anything being played this side of Neptune; it can also be a combination of well-known band styles. Some bands take imitation to the extreme, as in Crystal Ship's homage to The Doors. All are good approaches and give the new band many interesting musical options from which to choose.

Many rock bands assume a traditional setup: two electric guitars (rhythm and lead), electric bass, and trap drums. This configuration allows you to play just about any style of rock, from metal to folk rock. Metallica made thunder on that lineup. Sonic Youth created art-noise. Your parents may have stacks of LPs by four guys from Liverpool, England, who based their music on two guitars, bass, and drums. What was their name? The Buckles? The Bagels? Well, whatever . . . .

Some bands find fame, or notoriety, by playing the music of one style on the instruments of another. The band Run C & W may have a banjo and a washboard, but they love to play that sweet soul music, tongues firmly planted in their cheeks. During the late 1980s and early 1990s, the accordion waltzed out of the wedding band and into such rock lineups as Los Lobos and John Cougar Mellencamp's band. So keep an open mind. You may find a cellist who is not only a musical soulmate but also a metalhead; together you'll revolutionize the style.

Finding and Auditioning Players

Once you've decided what instruments you want, it is time to find the people to play them. As said before, you can begin by looking under your own roof. Family-based bands have their good and bad points. You might feel more comfortable, or be able to exchange creative ideas more easily, with a family member. Then again, you might drag family fights and rivalries into the band.

Local music store bulletin boards are a good place to put up signs advertising for musicians. If you're looking for a lead guitar player, a local music teacher might recommend a former or current student who happens to be a whiz at the style you are developing. Ask at local music stores or look under "Music/Instruction" in the Yellow Pages to find music teachers.

If you are in school, your music department is another good place to spread the word that you are looking for players. Ads in newspapers, especially school and "alternative" papers with younger readership, are a good idea. If you know someone already in a band, let him or her know of your quest for musicians. Even in a big city, music circles tend to be relatively small. Networking may be a concept you thought only applied to upwardly mobile business executives, but it works in the music business, too.

If you think a player might be right for the band you're forming, do what Van Halen did to find Sammy Hagar after David Lee Roth left: Hold an audition. Get together with the person and play a tune you both know. You'll be able to tell fairly quickly if the chemistry is right. Consider the player's ability level. If you plan on being your band's songwriter and rhythm guitarist and you audition a guitarist who plays circles around you, don't be intimidated. That player may fit nicely in your lead guitarist slot.

Try to see what a person can become, not just what she or he is at the time of the audition. Think twice before you say "Thanks, but no thanks" to the vocalist who sings flat once in a while but whose stage presence will electrify an audience. Problems like wavering intonation, sloppy playing, or uneven rhythm can be laid to rest if the person is willing to practice. And keep in mind, some people are terrific players because they spent hours in their bedrooms practicing. Unfortunately, the flip side is that those folks might be socially inept. Weigh the pros and cons of having an incredible player in the band who also might act like a nutcase from time to time.

Is Two Enough? Is Six Too Many?

Whether you're hanging back or in a hurry to find bandmates, consider how many people you want in the band. Years ago, the one-person band was a carnival act. An individual would strap a collection of clanking instruments to his or her body and by flicking wrists, flexing knees, and flapping elbows make, well, something like music. Today, technology such as drum machines and synthesizers makes it possible to be a band unto yourself. The artist formerly known as Prince created large chunks of his albums by himself. Nine Inch Nails is known for an industrial-style wall of sound; every musical brick was put there by one man, Trent Reznor.

Nevertheless, you are reading this book to start a band. If you hate crowds, think about forming a duo. Indigo Girls carved a distinctive sound with just two voices and two guitars. If two players can't make enough noise for you, consider a trio. During the 1980s, The Police made dense, layered pop with just Sting, Andy Summers, and Stewart Copeland.

The number of musicians in your band can grow to suit your ambitions. Frank Zappa and George Clinton had virtual mobs performing their pioneering funk, jazz, and rock fusions. If you've got a large sound in mind, recruit to your heart's content. But remember: the more players you have, the harder it may be to find places to play. Many music clubs have limited space. Six people in a band will give you that wall of sound, but makes for a lot of personalities to deal with, not to mention a skinnier cut when it comes to splitting up your hard-earned bucks. By the same token, a power trio is easier in terms of scheduling rehearsals and gigs but not as musically diverse.

The Name Game

You've lined up your players. Now it is time to think of a name. Of course the success of any band lives or dies on its music, but a great name never hurt any group's chances for fame and fortune. Coming up with a band name is actually harder than you might think. If you have five people in a band, you'll probably have five different opinions on any given suggestion. Don't wait to name yourselves; if you are rehearsing and talking up the band to friends, the time to name is now. You can't promote your band without a name.

The kind of music you play will help you pick a name. If you're called Embalming Fluid, chances are you're some kind of death metal band. If you play funk, a label like Groove Doctors will advertise your style. Whatever name you pick, everyone in the band should like it, because that name is going to become a part of you. Name-changing every three months makes it hard to promote your band and hard for your audience to find you. All band names seem awkward in the beginning. The first few times you say your band's name in conversation may feel odd; after you've played some gigs and things are cooking, that name will sound as normal as the one on your birth certificate.

A band can run into trouble if there is profanity or an objectionable word in its name. You won't get the gig if club owners or school dance committees love your music but are too angry or embarrassed to print your name on promotional materials. Artists have always dealt with the struggle between expressing themselves in ways that may not be commercially viable and garnering enough popular support to continue their art. If your name or material offends some people, be prepared to deal with the consequences of that choice. Then again, your goal may be to offend, so knock yourself out! That strategy worked for the Sex Pistols.

Pick a name that is easy to say and remember. The artist formerly known as Prince changed his name to an unpronounceable symbol. When you get as big as the guy who used to be known as Prince, you can do that sort of thing. For now, find a name that sticks in people's minds, then rolls off the tongue, especially in response to the question "Who's the greatest band in the universe?"

With all that said, ultimately it's the music that counts. A so-so name isn't going to keep you from your date with destiny if the chops or skills are there. John, Paul, George, and Ringo may have revolutionized pop music in the sixties, but the name of their band was pretty lame. Now what *was* that name . . . ?

Band Goals

after you've found the name that is going to capture the imagination of your soon-to-be adoring public, it's a good idea to talk about what everyone wants from the band. Granted, this may seem like an English assignment: Compare and contrast your hopes and dreams with the hopes and dreams of your bandmates.

Still, it's amazing what misconceptions and miscommunications can occur, even when you think you're all on the same wavelength. It's important to know that your guitar player harbors a secret desire to play country when you are trying to start a rock band. And what about group goals? Do you just want to play locally, or do you eventually want to tour and take the music as far as it will go? Amazingly enough, not everyone wants more fame than they know what do with. According to many, Kurt Cobain didn't want the international fame thrust upon him when Nirvana outsold Michael Jackson. They say he would have been happier having his band open up for other alternative bands like Sonic Youth. Some claim that the sudden fame, as well as drugs and other personal problems, drove him to suicide in 1994 at age twenty-seven.

Power Plays

most agree that Cobain, as singer, main songwriter, and guitarist, *was* Nirvana. What about the power structure of your band? That question may seem as if it should come from a corporate executive, but all groups of people, from bands to bird-watchers, have power structures. It'll help to know what yours is. If your band is called Little Johnny One-Eye and the BB Guns, you're probably a band led by Little Johnny. Little Johnny calls the shots, hiring and firing band members, determining material, fronting the band, booking gigs, and generally presiding over the BB Guns. Little Johnny can do this because he is also the draw. Fans line up to see him do whatever he does; they don't care if there is a revolving door for side musicians.

The benefit of this kind of band is that, if you, as a side person, show up on time and know your parts, that's mostly what is expected of you. The burden of getting gigs and pushing the name rests solely on the shoulders of Little Johnny. And if you happen to be the Little Johnny of your band, you may have all the stress of making the band work. But then you get all the glory.

If you are the official leader in your band, you tend to have most of the creative fun. If, however, you are a side person in this type of band, you may not be as creatively fulfilled, depending on the personality of the leader. It's frustrating when you keep coming up with great musical ideas and Little Johnny is just too blind in his one good eye to see your genius.

The other basic type of power structure in a band is the democratic approach. In the democratic approach, everyone has an equal voice in band politics. Band topics are discussed at large and decided on by consensus. This approach makes for lively discussions (and maybe some chair-throwing) and should lead to generous amounts of compromise. In an idealistic world, this is the one-player, one-vote strategy; in reality, as the old saying goes, some people are more equal than others. It's human nature that in any given group, some people will have stronger personalities (or right hooks) than others. Many times the democratic approach doesn't quite live up to its name. But the give-and-take of this kind of band usually lays fertile ground for collaborating on songs, a good thing for any band.

In the final analysis, the democratic approach is the only true band approach and is one reason why there are more single performers than bands. Getting a group of people, all talented and crazy in their own ways, to come together and focus on what is good for the music is a task that makes lesser bands blow apart like an egg hitting the pavement.

chapter two

Reflections and Shadows:
Cover and Original Music

You start out with a shadow, or an idea, and come up with something that's a shadow of that. You might like it better. It's still not exactly what you picture in your head, though.[1]

Axl Rose is describing the delicate process that created the sometimes indelicate sound of Guns 'n' Roses: songwriting. What types of songs will your band play? All of your decisions about instruments, direction, and musicians won't mean much if, at your first rehearsal, you're all plugged in with nothing to play.

The musical shadow-boxing Axl refers to is often involved in making original music. Not every band, however, chooses to write and perform self-penned tunes, especially at the outset. The next step in your band's rock and roll odyssey is to decide whether to play cover or original music.

Cover Music

If, as Axl says, original music involves playing with shadows, cover music is a game of reflections. Cover material means songs made popular by other bands or performers. Working on other performers' songs is a great way to get your chops together. Listening to and playing songs or solos over and over, though occasionally frustrating, expands your repertoire of chords and licks.

Listen carefully for musical subtleties in the songs you want to cover. If you decide to cover a "classic" rock tune like the Rolling Stones' "Brown Sugar," pick a detail downplayed in the original to accentuate in your version. Do you hear the acoustic guitar just below the electric? What about an all-acoustic rendition? Check out material from bands that are big on complex but hidden delights. Try to hear what bands are doing that is clever but not immediately obvious. Developing "big ears" is a fundamental part of becoming a good musician.

Playing a variety of cover material is a good way to find your own style, should you decide to try songwriting in the future. Infuse cover songs with your own creativity. Use of interesting arrangements, different time signatures or dynamics, or unusual instrumentation are just a few ways to make cover songs your own. And don't worry. Axl isn't going to send the song police after you if you have fun with one of his tunes. In fact, Guns 'n' Roses recorded a disc's worth of covers of classic punk tunes called *The Spaghetti Incident.*

Fortunately for bands, paying for the legal right to cover Axl Rose's, or anybody's, material lies with the people who hire them. Any establishment that has music for entertainment, be it live or recorded, has to pay an annual fee to BMI or ASCAP for a blanket license. BMI, Broadcast Music Incorporated, and ASCAP, the American Society of Composers, Authors and Publishers, are performing rights societies that keep track of when songs are played on radio and television and pay royalties to artists for that use. Because it would be a bookkeeping nightmare, establishments don't record every time a band covers a song; the blanket license takes care of any covered material a band might play.

Playing cover music can help a band get off the ground. On the local level, many people like to hear songs they are familiar with, making it easier for a band to establish a following. The bigger your following, the more clout you'll have in booking, but more on that in Chapter Five.

The lifeblood of most cover bands is the party, be it frat kegger, street dance, or twenty-first-birthday blowout. Often a cover band will give its song list to the hiring person, who then chooses the numbers she or he most wants to hear. If the hiring person is older, he or she might want to hear more tunes from the sixties and seventies; a younger hiring person might prefer more up-to-date covers. Being able to meet the needs of different situations will greatly increase your gig potential. But be careful; you can't be all things to all people. Don't say you can play mellow background music just to cash in on a juicy paying gig when, in reality, you're a bunch of headbangers.

The downside of being a cover band is that your versions will inevitably be compared to the originals. If your renditions are strong, no problem. If they're not, you'll be playing to empty chairs, while people stay at home grooving on their boom boxes.

More than a few bands get their start by engaging in the time-honored tradition of covering tunes from non-mainstream sources, or from years (and usually decades) past. Eric Clapton dug into his own past by reinventing his 1970 Derek and the Dominos classic "Layla" as an acoustic blues-rock ballad. To the twenty-five-and-under set, it was a completely new tune; to older folk, it was a fresh interpretation of an already great song.

Mexican folk music is not exactly considered mainstream, but when Ritchie Valens covered "La Bamba" in 1958, it stayed on the charts for weeks. In 1987, Los Lobos covered the same song and made it a hit all over again. In 1982, rocker Phil Collins took a trip to Motown and picked up a souvenir, his hit of the 1966 Supremes song "You Can't Hurry Love." Examples of performers covering older or obscure songs could fill a major city phone book. Check out those vintage record stores, garage sales, Uncle Herman's LP collection, or music conventions when they roll into town. You never know what gold you may find.

When deciding whether to play cover or original music, think about how far you want to go with your band. A cover band may pack 'em in till the dawn's early light but won't get much interest from record companies. If you eventually want to play more concertlike dates for a larger audience, original music is the way to go.

Original Music

the biggest plus in playing original music is that the songs are uniquely your own. If folks want to boogie to your latest red-hot number, they're going to have to show up at your gigs to do so. And usually, the original version of a song is considered the definitive one, although every rule has its exceptions. Otis Redding may have written "Respect," but everyone knows it's Aretha Franklin's song.

If you've decided to play original material, the band might have a harder time getting gigs at first, again assuming that people like to hear familiar songs. Still, people do like to hear new music; if they didn't, there wouldn't be this trillion-dollar mania called the music business. If you can generate excitement with original material, you align yourself with the pros on radio or MTV. Not bad company for someone just starting out. Protecting your songs with copyrights becomes more important when you decide to record those songs (see page 105 for more on obtaining a copyright).

Songwriting

riting a song is not difficult; writing a good song is. Picking out favorite songs to cover is like being a kid in a candy store—there are plenty of appealing choices. But writing fresh new songs is a craft that takes time to master.

Songwriting is a topic worthy of its own book. A few notable ones that have been written are *Writing Down the Bones* by Natalie Goldberg, *Everything You Always Wanted to Know About Songwriting* by Cliffie Stone, and *You Can Write Great Lyrics* by Pamela Phillips Oland. Needless to say, there are as many different approaches to songwriting as there are styles of rock. A few basic principles, however, apply across the board. When writing a melody, remember the KISS principle. No, that doesn't mean putting on makeup and puckering up. It's short for "keep it simple, stupid." If a melody is crammed with notes that zoom all over the scale like a roller coaster, it probably won't be that memorable. Or singable, for that matter.

But melody isn't the only ingredient that makes songs great. Words are another. A simple melody combined with a catchy lyrical phrase is known as a hook. As the name implies, a hook snags the listener's attention. The chant "Dream On," from the Aerosmith song of the same name; "December boys got it bad," from Big Star's "September Gurls"; "you really got me," by the Kinks, are just a few memorable hooks.

Hooks often repeat or play off the song's title or occur in the chorus. In addition to being memorable in and of themselves, they also help the listener to identify the song and, naturally, the group that recorded it. Hooks, though, don't have to be word-oriented or occupy the chorus. Slash's guitar introduction to "Sweet Child O' Mine" is an example of a great instrumental hook that identifies the song immediately.

Say you've got a unique melody and a catchy phrase for your chorus. Does that mean your song is an instant classic? Not quite. You'll want to surround that hook with verses that are just as inspiring. Clever lyrics can do the same job as a hook-filled chorus in prompting the listener to recognize a song. Throughout the ages, singers and poets have made their work recognizable through memorable melody and lyric phrases.

The lyrics of most songs are rhymed. Analyzing songs is an excellent way to understand how rhymes are made. Some rhyme AABB, meaning the first two lines rhyme (AA), as do the second two (BB). You can rhyme ABAB, AAB AAB, ABB ABB—a virtual alphabet soup of possibilities. And that's before you even get to the bridge.

A good tool to use for making interesting rhymes is a rhyming dictionary. A rhyming dictionary, not surprisingly, groups words by rhymes. Suppose you want to rhyme the word "say." Look in the A section for the long "a" sound or ā. (See, all that phonetic stuff you learned in school is coming in handy.) Some of the rhymes for "say" that easily come to mind are "day," "may," and "stay." But how about "ricochet?" Or "runaway?" Or even "negligée?" A rhyming dictionary can spice up your lyrics considerably while helping you avoid rhyming clichés. If you had a dollar for every time "love" and "above" have been rhymed, you could retire to Tahiti.

Another kind of rhyme is the interior rhyme. The interior rhyme pairs words throughout the line, not only ending words of different lines. This kind of rhyme gives a swinging feel to a song. Going back to the word "say," you could also use the words "take," "age," and "praise," and all of their rhyming words, to make your rhyme. Rhyming vowel sounds greatly increases the pool of words from which to choose.

Songwriting is like playing an instrument (and yes, the voice is an instrument). You have to practice to excel. Keep an open mind, have fun, and don't be too hard on yourself at first. After you've been writing a while, then it's time to be your own toughest critic. One way to do that is to record your songs. A hand-held cassette recorder will do the job. It is difficult to be objective about a song while you are singing it. Recording a song allows you time for objectivity, which can be hard to find in the creative process.

Speaking of the creative process, you might want to check out the work of the father of rock lyrics, even if it means—horror!—digging into your parents' records. Bob Dylan revolutionized the role of lyrics in rock music on such records as *Highway 61 Revisited*, *Blonde on Blonde*, *Blood on the Tracks*, and numerous others. Dylan's lyrics have influenced nearly everyone who has picked up a pen and a pick, from Keith Richards to Eddie Vedder of Pearl Jam, who sang Dylan's "Masters of War" at a concert celebrating his music.

Two Heads Can Be Better Than One

Writing songs with another person can be a good way to create memorable music. Maybe you have melodies flying out of your ears, but words come like molasses in January. Or possibly you scribble down lyrics on any available napkin or junk-mail envelope, hoping a tune will follow. Finding a partner who complements your writing style can be a boon to both of your songwriting abilities.

But you don't have to follow a strict "you write the words, I write the music" format. Many tunesmiths just keep fooling around with ideas, chords, and melodies. Some of the world's most cherished music has come out of the give-and-take of two songwriters working together toward the common goal of a song.

Years after the Beatles (that's it!) broke up, John Lennon shed some light on how he and Paul McCartney—perhaps rock music's greatest songwriting duo—collaborated:

> We wrote a lot of stuff together one-on-one, eyeball to eyeball. Like in "I Want to Hold Your Hand," I remember when we got the chord that made the song. We were in Jane Asher's [McCartney's girlfriend at the time] house, downstairs in the cellar playing on the piano at the same time. And we had, "Oh you-u-u . . . got that something. . . ." And Paul hits this chord and I turn to him and say, "That's it!" I said. "Do that again!"[2]

No matter how you set up your songwriting relationship, here are some points to keep in mind:

> Stay open. The point in collaboration is that the other person has a different personality and life experience to draw from; hence his or her

ideas will be different from yours. Allow yourself and your songwriting partner the freedom to explore.

Know that you will share credit when you write together. If someone gives his or her advice on a few lines of the chorus or the melody of the verses, you may not have to share credit. This area gets sticky because a few small suggestions can end up substantially changing a song. If that song goes on to be a hit, either by your band or a more well-known artist, nasty conversations about the song's ownership can ensue. Be up front about your expectations in regards to sharing credit.

Get copyrights on your songs (more about this in Chapter Six). If you just wrote the words and your musical partner just wrote the music, neither of you can use the song without the permission of the other. Copyrighting becomes more crucial when original songs are recorded, either by your band or another artist.

Not every song that comes out of your collaboration will be a keeper. Don't worry if you aren't inspired or your songwriting bud comes up empty trying to find lyrics for your melody. Collaboration is a tool to be used for songwriting; if it's not working, leave it for a while.

Stay flexible with your songwriting partner. If you want to write by yourself or with another person, do so. If your first partner wants to do the same, don't interpret the move as being dumped. The songwriting relationship is both creative and commercial. You and your partner are in the business of writing songs. Being imaginative while keeping an eye on the business aspects of collaboration can be tricky but is usually worth the effort.

Songwriting Groups

Many cities have songwriting groups, collections of people who want to share the trials and tribulations of putting together words and music. Call local music stores or the musicians' union to find out if your area has one of these organizations. Writing songs can be a lonely, frustrating activity. Songwriters' groups are a great place to trade ideas, strategies, and war stories about this most maddeningly satisfying activity. If you live in a small town that doesn't have such an organization, consider placing an ad in the local newspaper to start an informal group. You may find just the person to help you with the pesky second verse that is keeping you up at night. If you're a traveler on the information highway, you might also look for songwriting groups on the Internet.

Hot Topics

hen it comes to song topics, love or the lack thereof tops the charts of favorite things to write and sing about. In reality, any topic is fair game. The Japanese band Shonen Knife wrote beautifully simple songs about eating chocolate bars, sleeping, and taking baths. Whatever you feel passionate about, inspired by, or angry at can make a good song. How you treat your subject matter is ultimately more important than the topic itself. Challenge yourself with different kinds of songs: a heart-wrenching ballad, a comic ditty about your first date, a protest song describing your complete lack of desire to learn trigonometry.

Love as the number one song topic will be with us until the last note has been played. Still, it's a welcome change of pace to hear lyrics that aren't in the "oo baby, I want you, need you, love you," realm. Writing songs about people who affect you, whether you could hug or strangle them, has always been a mainstay for songwriters. Songwriters are inspired by books, news stories, relationships, and other musicians; find out what makes you want to put words to music. And, of course, a song doesn't have to have words. Trying to put across a feeling, mood, or attitude without the benefit of words makes writing instrumental music all the more challenging.

The Intro Bone Is Connected to the Verse Bone

fter working out the basic structure of a song, you need to arrange it. As the songwriter, you will have ideas about how you want the song to sound; your band members will also give suggestions on the arrangement of the song during rehearsal.

At the risk of being obvious, begin arranging at the beginning. Do you want the song to kick off with the vocalist singing a cappella, meaning without instruments? Or maybe the guitar and keyboards playing in harmony? Or how about a steady beat on the kick drum with a bass line on top? The possibilities don't stop there. If you have more than one vocalist, who will sing the lead? Who will sing harmony and during which parts? Will the harmony singers sing what the lead vocalist is singing, or will they sing different words or sounds in the background? And then there's the ending. Like the beginning, it should be well thought out and make sense in the song as a whole. As a basic rule, a simple tune can take more arranging. A complex tune, one with a lot of chords or words, tends to do better with a simpler arrangement. Again, go back to your music collection and listen to how songs are arranged. As you can see, the only thing that limits the arrangements of your songs is your own imagination.

Keep in mind that all of the musicians on your tapes or CDs had the freedom to arrange material that comes with a studio environment. Professionals can have orchestras in the background, bring in a variety of instrumental soloists, and play with effects, to name a few studio possibilities. But more on recording in Chapter Five. Still, listening to how other bands have arranged material will give you ideas for your own tunes.

Variety Is the Spice of Music

Strive for a variety of sound when writing and arranging your material. Too much of one kind of song or sound can be fatal. You may love those cry-in-your-pillow songs, but unless you're playing to a crowd that likes a good bummer, combine both upbeat and melancholy material.

A good mix of material means fast and slow tempos, songs played in a variety of keys, different time signatures, funny and straight material if you are humorously inclined, and a variety of dynamics. Dynamics means the varying levels of volume in any given song. Bringing a song to a whisper can be as dramatic as playing it to thundering decibels. If every song is cranked up to 11, the audience's lasting impression of your band might be that of a colossal headache. Consider the dynamics of your favorite tunes. Does tempo shift? Do the songs start quietly, then become loud? Led Zeppelin's classic "Stairway to Heaven" popularized a slow-to-fast, soft-to-loud progression, the influence of which can be heard on Guns 'n' Roses' "November Rain," Metallica's "One," and countless others.

Mix and Match

Many bands play both cover and original music—more cover at first to get established, then adding original music to explore personal creativity. This approach keeps the "play the hits" folks happy while satisfying the audience that wants to hear something new. If the mix you have works, don't change a winning game; if it doesn't, play around with your set list until you find the best combination of cover and original material. During the seventies, Eddie Van Halen fronted a popular party band in Los Angeles until the crowds wanted to hear his original material more than "Satisfaction" or "Louie, Louie."

When arranging songs and creating your repertoire, use anything you can think of to vary your sound while remaining true to your original style. The only way you can tell if your songs and arrangements work is in rehearsal. And the only way to do that is by having a public address system (P.A.).

chapter three

Bring the Noise: The P.A.

Halfway though the fifth number, "Off the Hook," police turned on the house lights and cut off the power to the amps and mikes. Charlie kept on drumming and Mick continued singing and playing maracas, with Brian [Jones] on tambourine and Keith and Bill clapping. When police refused to turn on the group's current, Mick apologized to the audience, said a few parting nasties to the cops, and they left the stage after a show that lasted fifteen minutes . . . Local papers gave the Stones their first sensational headline of the tour: POLICE QUELL RIOT AT ROLLING STONES CONCERT; CRUDE AND RUDE ROLLING STONES HURL INSULTS AT POLICE. ROLLING STONES CREATE HAVOC AT GARDENS— DAMAGES IN THOUSANDS REPORTED.[1]

As this tale of an early Rolling Stones concert proves, the importance of a band's P.A. should not be underestimated. With a P.A., you can be the world's greatest rock band, dazzling fans who've flocked from miles. Without it, you can be the world's greatest rock band sending those same fans home disappointed.

Short for public address, a P.A. is the collection of equipment that amplifies the sound level of a performance so it can be heard in a large space. A P.A. also allows an electric band to rehearse in a small setting.

So far, you've cleared the first several hurdles to forming a band—getting people together, agreeing on a musical direction, and choosing songs. Aquiring a P.A. is one of the toughest hurdles yet to be scaled. For most bands, a P.A. is bank-breaking to buy and back-breaking to haul. Some bands avoid the hassle; fully-equipped rehearsal studios rent time to bands. Rehearsal studios usually have rooms of varying sizes, smaller rooms costing from $8 to $10 an hour, larger rooms going for up to $20 an hour. Rehearsal studios tend to be in mid- to large-sized cities, unfortunately so for bands based in rural areas. And many music clubs have a house P.A. But having a P.A. at your disposal, either bought by the band or a single band member, greatly increases your chances for regular rehearsal sessions and gigs and, therefore, that all-too-elusive fame and fortune.

The P.A.

I f you want to know in scientific terms how a P.A. works, read *Sound Reinforcement Handbook* by Gary Davis and Ralph Jones.

Sound reinforcement is the technical term for amplification through a public address system. *Sound Reinforcement Handbook* is the bible of P.A. systems. It delves into the nature of sound, electricity, and electronics but is, at times, difficult to understand, especially for those who just barely passed math and science. Nevertheless, it contains information that the lay person can use. Most bands develop a love/hate relationship with their P.A.s: They love the power of being able to reach so many people at one time, but hate the inevitable hissing, popping, humming, feedback, and occasional outright system failure. Any book that can help your relationship with the P.A. be more of the former and less of the latter is worth searching for in your local library or adding to your bookshelf.

All P.A.s, whether being used by your principal to address the school assembly or Aerosmith to kick start a crowded stadium, are basically the same. The fundamental parts of a P.A. are the microphones, mike stands, power amplifier, mixing board, monitor system, speakers, and cables.

Microphones

icrophones, or mikes, are the equipment that changes voice or instrumental sound into an electrical signal that travels down the mike cord, through the mixing board, to the power amp, then out the speakers as amplified sound. The cost of a mike runs from sixty dollars all the way to thousands of dollars.

There are two basic kinds of mikes: dynamic and condenser. A dynamic mike picks up sound from a small surrounding area. A singer can close in on a dynamic mike and usually not cause feedback because the mike is less sensitive. Feedback is a frequency buildup in the P.A. system. For example, a vocalist sings a note into a mike. That note comes out of the main speakers and is picked up again by the singer's mike. The mike puts the sound back in to the P.A., which puts the sound back out the speakers to be picked up again by the mike and so on, creating a sound loop. That loop builds to the point of overload, creating the all-too-familiar screech. The sound person should find the input that is mixed too high and bring it down to a level where the feedback doesn't occur. Usually feedback is caused by the arrangement of the mikes and main or monitor speakers. Make sure the speakers are not aimed directly at the microphones. Dynamic mikes have a higher gain before feedback ratio, gain meaning the level of the electrical signal that translates into volume. A dynamic mike can take a lot of sound or signal before it starts to squeal.

Condenser mikes contain mini-amplifiers, giving them a lower gain before feedback ratio. This ratio means the mike tends to feed back when the singer or player gets too close. Generally, condenser mikes work best with instruments; if you are playing an acoustic guitar, stay a few inches away from the mike in order for the resonant sound of the guitar to form in front of the mike. Hung over a trap set, a condenser mike will pick up the entire set, not just the cymbals.

Most condenser mikes have what is called an omnidirectional polar pattern, meaning the mike will pick up sound from any direction. In contrast, most dynamic mikes are cardioid in their polar patterns, meaning the area for picking up sound is limited to right in front of and to the side of the mike. Lead singers tend to want a cardioid polar pattern because they don't want the guitar sound bleeding into their vocal mike. Your band will need a mike with an omnidirectional polar pattern if the harmony singers intend to use one mike.

When shopping for a new mike, tell the sales-person in the music store what the mike will be used for. If it is for a vocalist, is that person male or female? One kind of mike will handle the lower register of a male singer; another will better suit the higher female voice. The same idea follows for instruments: If the mike is to be used for a violin, be sure it is suited to a good treble response.

Even though they are made of metal, don't be fooled: Mikes are delicate and must be handled with care. You might have seen a rock star swing-ing his or her mike by the cord like a cowboy about to lasso a stray. What you don't see is the sound person tearing out his or her hair over the fate of a valuable piece of equipment. Don't try the swing-ing routine unless you have a rock star's income and can go through mikes like tissue paper. It costs as much to fix a mike as it does to replace it, so try not to have fumble fingers. Mikes when not being used should always go back in the box or case they came in.

Many vocalists like to have windscreens on their mikes. A windscreen is the foam covering that fits snugly over the mike, preventing it from picking up wind noise or popping "p" sounds from the singer. Some vocalists don't like wind-screens because, depending on the kind of mike, a windscreen can take off some of the vocal's highs and lows. Many mikes have built-in windscreens, making the foam kind unnecessary.

Microphone Technique

Mike technique is the way a vocalist sings into a mike. Good mike technique helps the vocal to sound relaxed but strong, soft when the song calls for it, wailing when it's time to cut loose. What is good mike technique? Basically, it means setting the gain level of the mike to the vocalist's advantage and the vocalist judging how close he or she can sing into that mike in order to get the desired vocal sound. If you don't have a windscreen and your p's are exploding like popcorn, move a few degrees to the right or left of the mike to avoid a head-on presentation. Hold the mike with your fingertips; gripping a mike like a baseball bat gives you less control of your mike and is tiring for your hand.

If you have to "eat the mike" or have your lips on the mike in order to be heard over the instruments, turn up that input. If the mike feedbacks, turn down the players. Eating the mike tends to make the vocal boomy. Many times, changing the equalization (EQ) or tonality of the mike, increasing the treble, or rolling off the bass can make a vocalist cut through the backup players without increasing the vocalist's volume. Experiment with vocal mike levels in order to find the optimal setting.

Microphone Stands

The mike sits in the holder of a mike stand. There are two basic types of mike stands: the round base and the tripod stand. Accessories screw into the stand. What you are using the mike for will help to determine your best stand and accessory combination.

The heavy round base with rubber feet is the cheapest kind of stand and comes in two weights: 10 and 25 pounds (4.5 and 11.3 kilograms). The heavy base gives good stability to the stand—a necessity, considering it is holding a precious piece of equipment. The round base takes up less room, an important consideration when playing those postage-stamp-size stages. If you are playing on a makeshift plywood stage, toe-tapping and walking around become noise that can find its way into the P.A. A heavy round stand absorbs a lot of unwanted sound. The tripod is a three-legged stand and usually costs more than the round base. These two kinds of stands come with a straight metal pole with the mike clip at the top or a variety of accessories.

The two main kinds of mike stand accessories are the boom and the gooseneck. The boom can be a single arm that fixes at an angle to the straight pole or a telescoping boom that can adjust from 2 to 3.5 feet (0.6 to 1 meter) from the metal pole. The telescoping boom is an especially effective mike stand setup because it gives the musician playing or singing ample body space. Lemmy, the driving force behind Motörhead, favored an unusual boom setup—extending the boom at a slight angle to the stand pole and dangling the mike in front of his face.

The gooseneck is a flexible metal accessory that allows the mike to be put in a variety of positions. This feature may make the gooseneck seem like the best kind of accessory; in reality, a gooseneck will lose its flexibility over time, meaning it won't stay where you put it. When that happens, you basically have a useless accessory.

A less frequently used kind of stand is the desk, or short stand. This stand is less than a foot high and is used to mike an amp or floor toms on a trap set.

Microphone Cords

A microphone cord snaps into the mike at one end and into the mixing board at the other, carrying the electrical signal from the mike to the mixing board. Surprisingly, you have to take as much care with mike cords as you do with the mikes themselves. Inside the mike cord is a braided copper grounding wire. This grounding wire takes out the unwanted electricity that translates to the P.A. system as buzzes, hisses, hums, and a host of other electrical gremlins. If the copper grounding wire breaks, the whole cable is shot. Always buy new mike cables, which run about a dollar a foot. And buy brand names. There are areas in which you can save a buck or two when buying your P.A.; mike cords isn't one of them.

When buying cords, ask your salesperson to show you the lariat wrap. This wrap is the correct way to wrap a mike cord so that the copper braid inside lies flat and does not become damaged. The over-the-shoulder-and-under-the-elbow wrap is eventual death for a mike cord; band members caught doing this wrap should be forced to listen to elevator music for eternity. To keep your cords correctly coiled, use a Velcro wrap, or the ties that come with plastic garbage bags. Or borrow some of your little sister's hair ties, the kind with the plastic balls that loop around each other. When it comes to wrapping any kind of wire or cord, neatness counts. If you don't secure wrapped cords, your cord box or bag will resemble a nest of snakes.

Be sure to plug in and pull out cables by the metal housing. You will destroy the wiring inside if you pull out a cord by the plastic covering. For instrument cords, make sure your metal covering is screwed in correctly. Many musicians prefer instrument cords with copper tips that make for a better electrical connection.

The Mixing Board

all the inputs from the mikes and instrument amps plug into the mixing board. The electrical signals generated in the mikes and amps travel to the mixing board, where the signals are adjusted in terms of volume and tone control or bass and treble. The mixing board makes either stereo or monaural sound. Monaural boards mix all the inputs into one signal, then split the signal equally between both speakers. Stereo boards also combine all the inputs, then split the signal between the two speakers. But a stereo system will have slightly more of some inputs coming out of one speaker and slightly more of the rest coming out of the other.

The mixing board also has a control called a pan pot, which fixes the sound in relation to the two speakers. If the pan pot is all the way to the left, the sound will come out of the left speaker. If it is all the way to the right, the sound will come out of the right speaker. For most gigs, it is best to have the sound equally balanced between the two speakers.

Most mixing boards have effects loops that add enhancements to the sound. One effect used frequently is called reverb. Reverb (short for reverberation) simulates the way sound bounces around the reflective surfaces in a room. How much reverb to use depends on whether you want, for example, the effect of your vocalist singing in a large hall, a medium-sized club, or an intimate coffeehouse. In terms of reverb, you can play anywhere from your bathroom to the Taj Mahal. Some bands prefer a "dry" sound, meaning no reverb on the vocals. Other bands experiment with different levels of reverb on instruments. How much reverb you want depends solely on what sounds good to your ear. It is hard to imagine the music of the Pixies, or that of their music mentors, The Ventures, without reverb.

The Power Amplifier and Speakers

In less expensive P.A. systems, the power amplifier is often built into the mixing board. The power amplifier enhances the electrical signal coming from the mikes and amps. The capability of a power amp is determined by its wattage number; the higher the wattage number, the more volume can be put through the speakers and the more expensive the power amp. The power amp is the workhorse of the system and is probably the component that will last the longest. As your band changes over time, you might need a different mixing board, new mikes, or replacements for blown speakers. The power amp, however, is the closest thing in the P.A. system to a onetime purchase.

Buy speakers that can handle the wattage of the power amp. A high wattage power amp putting signals through cardboard speakers will produce poor quality sound. Likewise, it doesn't help to have top-of-the-line speakers if you have a low wattage amp.

The speakers, connected to the power amp by speaker wires, mark the end of the road for the electrical signal. Like the mikes, the speakers do not actually amplify the sound. Instead they allow the electrical signal to leave the system in a way that translates as louder sound. Most inexpensive P.A.s have speakers with a 15-inch (38-centimeter) woofer to handle the bass range and a 1-inch (2.5-centimeter) horn for the treble end. Speakers also have what is called a crossover network. This network keeps the bass range from going through the horn and vice versa. When setting up your P.A., remember to keep the speakers in front of the mikes to avoid a feedback loop.

If you have more ambition than money, buy a good how-to book and build your own speakers. It will help to have some woodworking and electrical knowledge to undertake this task. Building your own speakers will save you a chunk of money over buying ready-made speakers. If you decide to go this route, follow the instructions carefully and ask for help when necessary. If the speakers don't work, you'll end up with two big wooden boxes with components in them, suitable for bedside tables.

The Monitor System

the monitor system is actually an entire sound system in itself that is usually part of the mixing board/power amp unit. This system allows the performers to hear themselves through speakers, or monitors, that are on the stage. A good monitor system is essential to a band because it is the only way a band hears itself. If players can't hear themselves, they sing or play off, making both band and audience suffer in the process. The mix of the monitors is different from the mix that is going through the main speakers. In some P.A. systems, monitors can be adjusted so that players can hear themselves more in the speaker that is closest to them.

Watch out for the "more me" syndrome when mixing the band's monitors. The guitar player turns up, so the bass player follows suit. Then the vocalist can't hear himself or herself sing and so on, until the situation deteriorates into screeching feedback or dirty looks being exchanged on stage. Practice monitor etiquette. Find the balance between hearing yourself enough so that you can comfortably play and not being so loud as to drown out other players.

Mixing Your Sound

If your band has the money, think about hiring a sound person. A sound person helps set up and tear down the P.A. He or she also runs the P.A. while the band is performing. Mixing sound means adjusting the different levels so that they come together to form a cohesive sound—the sound of your band as a whole. In order for a sound person to do his or her job, the band must invest in what is called a snake. A snake is a large cable that brings all the signals from the P.A. to the mixing board, which is out in the audience. Having a person run your sound from the audience is the best way to get good sound, but with a sound person being another cut and a good snake starting at about $1,000, it is usually only a dream for the beginning band.

Because of financial considerations, most new bands mix their sound from the stage. The person who knows the P.A. best and who has an ear for what sounds good should run the mix. And it should be just one person. If everyone in the band tweaks knobs at will, the result will be uneven sound. The person mixing should learn the most effective volume level for the band and P.A. system. Too soft sound won't have the impact you want, too loud sound will blow out both eardrums and speakers. The mixer also needs to know what kind of vocal and instrumental quality the band wants to achieve. Making the singer sound natural and not distorted or grainy, or the guitar sound like a guitar, are skills that take time to master. The person mixing can run the main

P.A. System

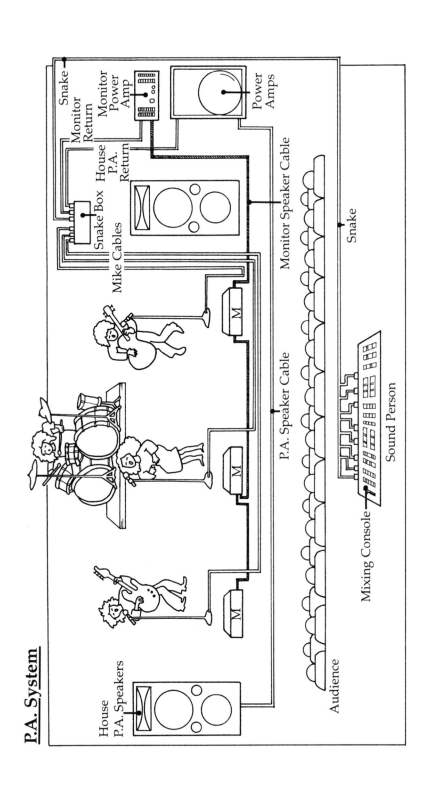

speaker mix through the monitors, allowing the band to hear what the audience hears.

Every place a band plays will have its own acoustics. The acoustics of a room are determined by the way sound reacts in the room, depending on the room's size, height of the ceiling, building materials, and so on. The P.A. has to be adjusted to fit the acoustics of each place. For example, if the band is playing in a cavernous hall that makes the P.A. sound boomy, the bass response should be rolled off in the mix. Be aware that every place you play will present its own acoustical challenges.

The Tuner

While not part of the P.A. system, the tuner is another essential piece of band equipment. With your assistance, the tuner tunes your instrument. A musician either plugs into a tuner and tunes electronically or tunes an acoustic instrument by matching a tone generated by the tuner. Tuning by ear is certainly a skill all musicians must have. Getting several instruments to be in tune with each other, however, can be a challenge for a new group. The best way to tune a band is with a tuner. Also, you want your band tuned to pitch, in the United States, A440 Hz. The vocalist might be affected if the band is tuned higher or lower than what he or she is expecting for the lead singing. Many times, plugging into your tuner is the only way to tune in a noisy club. If possible, set up your tuner on stage; if your instrument cannot be quickly tuned on stage, un-plug from the P.A. (turning down that input first!) and plug into the tuner. Stringed-instrument players should stretch out their strings while putting on a new set. Tuning is crucial. An out-of tune instrument can turn your terrific song into the musical equivalent of fingernails on a blackboard.

What to Buy

there are many different brands of P.A.s to choose from. When buying new, you pay more but get the warranty. If anything breaks down within the time period covered, you don't have to pay to get it fixed. Also, you have the support of the music store where you bought the equipment. If the manual seems like hiero-glyphics, the sales staff will be happy to translate for you.

You can also buy new equipment from a mail-order company and save from 10 percent to 50 percent, depending on what you buy. The catalogs from these companies are thorough and the phone sales people knowledgeable, but if you prefer more "hands on" help, buying from a retail store will be worth the extra cost in terms of product support.

Not surprisingly, used is cheaper than new equipment. Buying used equipment is also more time consuming. You have to scour the want ads in your local newspaper or music store bulletin board. Then you have to drive to the person's place to look over the stuff. When the mikes are in one place, speakers another, and power amp yet another, that's a lot of time spent on effort and gas. But the payoff is big when you piece together a solid P.A. without paying big bucks.

It helps to be knowledgeable about P.A. equipment in general before you buy used. And you should be able to trust the person selling you the equipment. That person may say it works fine; unfortunately, there are individuals in this world who would sell you bogus equipment and not feel even a twinge of guilt. If you are buying used equipment, be sure to get the manual and any record of repairs that have been done.

P.A. for a Day

Y ou or your band has decided to bite the financial bullet and buy a P.A. One way you can pay back on that investment is by renting the equipment to other bands. If the person renting your equipment is your life-long pal whom you would trust with a winning lottery ticket, just rent out the hardware. If, however, the person renting your equipment is a friend of a friend of a friend, include yourself in the deal as sound person, roadie, and equipment baby-sitter. You can increase the rental price if you are going to mix sound; nudging knobs for a band other than your own is a great way for you to get to know your P.A.

P.A. rental prices will vary across the country; one estimate in central Texas for a 6-channel board/power amp setup, with three mikes, monitor system, and main speakers was between $40 and $50 for 24 hours. That same P.A. configuration with a 12-channel board will run approximately $60 to $70.

Make sure your equipment is in top working order before you rent it out. Try to avoid the "that mike was busted when we got it out of the case" scenario. Both parties need to know in advance who will pay for a ripped speaker or mangled mike. And get your cash from the night's gig money. Bands come and go like the wind. It will be hard to collect from a broken-up band.

Going Mobile

having a P.A. is a great asset; you also must have a way of getting it to gigs or rehearsal space. A van is the traditional favorite as the band vehicle. The large square space in the back makes packing a P.A. relatively easy; the equipment can also be locked up and hidden from prying eyes. It's a good idea to lay a rug or piece of carpet on the van floor to minimize the inevitable scratches and dings to your equipment. When packing your P.A. make sure everything is secure. A monitor speaker in the back of the head when the van stops short can ruin your whole day.

If owning a van is not possible, split the transportation of the P.A. between whatever cars are available. You might run into trouble if band members drive econoboxes; if you have transportation problems, borrow a parent's or friend's more P.A.-

friendly vehicle for the evening. Or plan on making a few trips to the gig in your most suitable band car. Remember: A well-running vehicle is an essential part of your band's equipment; if your wheels aren't working, neither is your band.

Tearing Down

S etting up the P.A. is usually less of a drag because you have playing to look forward to. But tearing down can create friction in a band if only one or two people are doing the work of the entire band. It's normal to want to socialize with friends after a gig. But don't use schmoozing as an excuse to get out of wrapping cords and schlepping speakers. Unless your band has designated certain to do it, everyone should help tear down, making this unpleasant task at least a hair more tolerable.

chapter four

Practice, Practice, Practice: Rehearsal

Acting on the assumption that as a bigger band, they [Metallica] ought to try out professional accommodations at a "real" rehearsal studio, the group endured a short-lived stint at a Marin County rehearsal room.

"It was this place with real fancy, up-to-date. . . .[stuff]," recalled Lars in a fan club interview. "But there was no atmosphere. . . . I had a pretty big two-car garage. After all, the first three albums were written in a garage and, let's face it, in attitude, anyway, what more are we than a garage band?"

Instead of doing a ramshackle job of modifying their new hangout, the band invested considerable time and money on a professional soundproofing job. . . . [Then] they began "christening" the garage with a series of extended jam sessions.[1]

Metallica's search for the right rehearsal space in which to practice songs for their fourth album led them right back to where they had always played: a garage. True, their new space received some high-tech treatment, but it was still a garage.

Practicing in a garage has been a traditional favorite for most bands. Even when it's attached to a house, a garage is often far enough away from a home's other living spaces to allow non-rocking family members to be relatively undisturbed by bashing drums and crunching chords. But not always. If you're rehearsing in someone's garage, be aware of your volume level. Blasting decibels might sound good to you, but realize that not everyone in your family shares your need for noise. If a family member asks you to turn down, do so.

You can also avoid conflict by planning ahead. Can your band rehearse at times when the house is relatively empty? What about right after school? Afternoon practice sessions are easier on the ears and nerves of family members and neighbors than evening rehearsals. Folks are less likely to be trying to unwind after a long day or putting their children, not to mention themselves, to bed. If you can't find suitable rehearsal digs, check into renting a practice space.

The Ground Rules

no matter where you rehearse, decide on a few practice ground rules. Rehearsals will run smoother if you talk as a group about what is reasonably expected from each band member. Decide how many times a week you plan to rehearse. People will have other commitments; if you can only rehearse once a week, accept that as a limitation and make the most out of the time. Make a special effort to get to rehearsal. Saying you can't show because your favorite Abbott and Costello movie is on will guarantee you afternoons and evenings free from annoying disturbances like rehearsal, because you won't be playing in a band.

Rehearsal is just that. If you want to catch up on the latest news, plan to do so before or after rehearsal time. It is easy to go off on a tangent, talking about the latest Schwarzeneger flick; before you know it, twenty minutes are history. That doesn't mean you have to turn your rehearsal into a death march. A few conversational side trips can provide respite from a song that refuses to cooperate. Just don't lose too much precious rehearsal time to chitchat.

Remember the golden rule of rehearsal: Be on time for others as you would have them be on time for you. If rehearsal starts at seven, be there at seven. Nothing is more bothersome than having your drummer shuffle in an hour late, then having to waste time bringing her or him up to date. This hard-line approach may sound like—dare it be said—work, but that's what rehearsal sessions are. If you just want to get together and fool around with some tunes, fine. Being a band involves individual practice and band rehearsal. The player who can't take either of those things seriously is not worth keeping in the band, even if he or she is a monster player.

The Learning Curve

When it comes to rehearsal, remember the Boy Scout motto: Be prepared. Rehearsals will be more productive if band members learn chords and / or singing parts beforehand. Stumbling over chords you should have learned weeks ago won't endear you to your musical compadres. One good way for a band to learn a new song is for the person who knows or wrote the song to hand out copies of the song on cassette, along with charts (lyric sheets with chords written over the appropriate words). The tape and chart should be enough for the musicians to learn the basic song; in rehearsal, the band should be ready to play and arrange the song.

Keep charts of your tunes in a three-ring binder. Write notes about the songs' arrangements on the charts; if you haven't played a song in a while and can't remember if the 'oo' harmonies come in on the first or second verse, the chart will tell. Also, if your lead guitarist breaks his or her wrist and can't play for a couple of months, a practice tape and charts will help a fill-in player learn your material quickly.

What Do You Mean, I'm Singing Off?

Rehearsal sessions are the best times to look objectively at your music. Criticism is a touchy subject in any band. How a band deals with criticism can be an indicator of that band's life expectancy. If there isn't a reasonable exchange of ideas and opinions, the band won't grow—if it gets off the ground at all.

Giving effective criticism is an art form of the highest order. It takes some skill to critique someone's playing or songwriting without leaving them in shreds on the floor. One approach is to simply identify the line or lick that you think is awry. Many times just saying "What's your first chord on the second verse?" will be enough to let the person see it is a wrong chord. If that doesn't work, something like "I think that chord is supposed to be A minor, not A 7" will be infinitely more constructive than "No, you bonehead, A minor, A MINOR!"

Be specific. If one chord bothers you, comment on that chord. Don't give the impression you think the person is a lousy musician. Focusing on the specific problem and not the person helps everyone keep his or her self-respect. And choose your battles. If you criticize every little thing, people won't listen when you feel something is really important. Make sure that what you're commenting on is worth the trauma of bringing it up.

If the criticism is aimed at you, try to keep an open mind. A band is a collective endeavor. To that end, consider how the criticism helps the band. If the keyboard player sounds good, the band sounds good. If you as the vocalist need feedback, it is to help improve the sound of the band, not to rake you over the coals. Criticism of an individual aspect of a song is just that, not a blanket judgment of your worth as a person. Though difficult, it is best to hear criticism from your band members. If you don't, you'll hear it in the resounding echo of your music reverberating through empty clubs and dance halls.

One more thing about criticism. If a musician is struggling with a certain chord, lick, or vocal passage, be patient. Sometimes it is hard to get that difficult passage note-perfect the first, second, or even third time out. If you think the player will eventually improve, hold your tongue. Rehearsal is the place to experiment. If you never stretch yourself as an individual or as a band, you'll dig yourself into a predictable and ultimately boring rut. And if *you're* bored with the music, imagine how your audience will feel, if you can keep one.

Home Recording

maybe in the future, scientists will discover a way for musicians to develop two sets of ears. The first set will listen to the musician's playing, making sure it is on track. The second set will evaluate how that individual's playing fits into the band as a whole. Until that day comes, your band will have to rely on technology that is cruder, but no less effective: home recording. The best way to find out about your playing as a group is to record songs in your rehearsal sessions. Your recording equipment doesn't have to rival that of a sixty-four-track studio. A boom box that reproduces a clean sound will do. Listening to your band play and sing can be a humbling experience. But it is better to catch those wrong chords, off harmonies, or ill-fated arrangements before they hit the stage.

Listening to songs recorded in rehearsal makes individual practice more productive. Suppose the band takes an hour to arrange a song. After trying several different ways, you finally decide how you want to play it. But a week later, you can't quite dredge that arrangement from your memory. If you recorded the song, all you have to do to remember the arrangement is press the play button. Don't burn valuable rehearsal time by having to piece together previously arranged songs.

Taping songs in rehearsal will help you evaluate how each member's contribution fits into the band's overall sound. In terms of singing, the lead vocalist should be loud enough to be heard over the instruments but not so loud as to overpower them. The lead vocalist can cut loose on a melody, doing it a slightly different way each night. But for harmony singing, everyone needs to sing the same way each time. Harmony singers should blend their voices as much as possible, matching phrasing, or the way the lyrics are sung, breathing, tone, and so on. Boyz II Men, En Vogue, and UB40 are examples of bands with great vocal blends. Not surprisingly, many great harmony bands are composed of family members, supporting the notion that it takes years of singing together (with a little help from genetics) to get that terrific sound.

Enunciate when singing. People want to hear the words to songs, especially those you have written. Mushing over words just makes your songs sound like mush. True, many great singers have a growling, raspy delivery or a laconic approach that stretches out words like bubble gum. That's individual style, not general mush. You

might think your mumbling sounds are under-
standable because you know the words. But the
lyrics have to be clear enough to be understood
without sounding like an elocution lesson.

The music will suffer if the vocalist is developing golf-ball-sized vocal cord nodes from scream-
ing above a brain-piercing guitar level. It may feel
good to play as loud as you can, but it is not
always in the best interest of the band. People are
not just trying to rain on your parade by telling
you to turn down; they want the overall sound of
the band to be more balanced. Listening to yourself and the band at the same time takes practice,
but it is essential if a group ever wants to achieve a
band sound.

Rehearsal is the crucible in which your band is
formed. It is the time when all that matters is the
music. There is no stage, no audience, no buzz, no
distraction from the fundamental question: Does
our music say what we want to say in the way we
want to say it? If you can't get a thrill from just
playing with your bandmates, you may have
bought a one-way ticket to that great band burial
ground that is littered with the bleached bones of
countless groups that died in rehearsal.

chapter five

Playing Around:
Gigs and Promotion

Our sets progressed from ten minutes to twelve minutes. We did all the songs we knew. A lot of songs were very short and fast, so they just flew by. And then sometimes if a song didn't sound right, we'd have to stop and start again, you know, or argue with each other.[1]

So Joey Ramone recalled the first time he and his fellow Ramones played CBGB (short for country, bluegrass, blues), a bar in New York City's seedy Bowery. Its owner, Hilly Kristal, originally planned to book country bands.

Fortunately for the Ramones—and for rock and roll—Kristal didn't stick to his initial booking strategy. Other new bands followed the Ramones' footsteps across CBGB's sticky floors and onto its rickety stage. The bands had soon-to-be-familiar names: Blondie, Talking Heads, Patti Smith Group, Television, and many others.

A scene was born, and with it a new type of music: punk rock. Embracing styles that ranged from primitive, loud, and fast—the Ramones' "blitzkrieg bop"—to sophisticated combinations of music and poetry—the Patti Smith Group's sound—punk rock went on to influence two generations of listeners. In London, the Sex Pistols heard the Ramones and began creating their own outrageous, political music. A decade later, in Aberdeen, Washington, a high school misfit named Kurt Cobain heard punk and said: "Punk is musical freedom. It's saying, doing and playing what you want. In Webster's terms, nirvana means freedom from pain, suffering and the external world, and that's pretty close to my definition of punk rock."[2]

Quite an accomplishment for a sound that got its start in a dive. But it shows what is possible in rock and roll with even the humblest beginning. You're probably thinking: What chance has my band got of being part of a new movement in music? The answer is: You'll only find out by getting out there and playing.

The Test Drive

before blazing new trails in music, you might want to road test your band for performing. A good way to do that is to have a party with the band as the main event. Invite your friends and tell them to invite their friends. Talk up the party and your band at school, church, the local recreation center, baseball diamond, or bowling alley. And talk about it with enthusiasm. If you aren't excited about your new group, no one else will be, either.

A party is a relaxed way for your band to break the ice and work toward that all-important first gig. Sounding good in rehearsal is a prerequisite for playing in public. But sounding good while performing for friends, family, and a few party-crashers will be tougher. Go a little easy on yourselves for that first performance. The only way to overcome the stress of performing is to perform. If things don't go exactly according to plan, don't chuck the whole band in the Dumpster. It takes time for things to jell on stage. Look at your party showcase as a kind of laboratory in which you are experimenting with your band's performance.

Stage Presence

Consider your band's stage presence. Are you having a good time, moving or dancing around, laughing, smiling, or generally getting down? Or do you exude the excitement of a mike stand? People like to hear live music to have a good time. That aspect might be in short supply if band members look like they've just come from a funeral. Playing music on stage is performing, like portraying a character in a play. True, you are playing yourself. But you are playing a certain version of yourself, that of the energetic musician. Even if you have a lousy cold or your main squeeze just found other lips to lock, try to act as though the show is all that matters.

An unpleasant factor of stage presence is stage fright. Stage fright can be that queasy feeling in the stomach, a tightening of the throat, knees like jelly, or sweaty palms. Being nervous is a significant part of performing to deal with; eventually nervousness can be overcome. Joni Mitchell and Van Morrison didn't play in front of audiences for years because of stage fright. Don't let butterflies cramp your style. Everyone is nervous in the beginning. The more you perform, the more comfortable you will feel on stage. Take deep breaths, remind yourself that you know the songs and that they sound good, and knock 'em dead.

Stage fright can destroy an important aspect of performing: concentration. You're not thinking about the music if you're worrying that your fly might be open. Nerves have a nasty habit of detouring your thoughts from the music at hand to the pit in your stomach. The best way to fight the fright is to concentrate on the music.

I Can't Believe I Blew That Chord

every performer, from the most exalted to the most lame, makes mistakes on stage. What separates the professional musician from the rest is that the pro has learned to flub a note or chord and get back on track immediately, making the mistake almost imperceptible. It is tempting to take a mental vacation to the Bahamas while performing a song you've played countless times. Your mind may be away, but your body is still on stage. It is difficult to recover from a mistake if you are on automatic pilot; all too easily, one blown chord can stretch into slicing and dicing the entire bridge. Stay with the song. Know where you are in it and where you are going. Save your mental vacations for when you really need them—in the dentist's chair.

Don't be too hard on yourself if you make mincemeat out of a tune. Tell the little voice inside your head that says "What a lamebrain! A two-year-old could play this song better" to take a hike. Everyone makes mistakes. If you are blowing a song because you don't really know it, make time to practice. If you are blowing it because you are spacing out, put more effort into staying in the present and concentrating on the music. If you are blowing it because you are nervous, know that everyone deals with performance fear; trust that eventually your hands will stop trembling and you will be able to play that song just the way you do in your living room. Remember, some amount of nerves is nature's way of keeping you on your toes.

The goal is not necessarily to get rid of the butterflies but to make them fly in formation with you as the squadron commander.

Talking on Stage

another important decision to make in developing your live act is who fronts the band. Many bands pick one person to talk to the audience; others like the interplay of the whole band putting in their two cents' worth. Whoever does the talking has two main functions:

to introduce songs and fill dead air, that awkward time when the silence on stage is deafening. If the guitar player is tuning for the umpteenth time, the front person should keep the audience's attention from wandering.

How much and what kind of stage patter you have will to some extent depend on what kind of band you are and the venue or gig itself. It is easier to chat about songs when playing in a small listening room. Likewise, it is hard to be intimate when the gig is set in a supermarket parking lot. If it is a dance gig, that's what folks want to do, not listen to lengthy introductions.

Every date is different; learn to evaluate your audience's fidget factor for stage talk. A cover band introducing an original song can kick in the audience's thirst, creating a mass exodus for refreshments. Play your original tune without introducing it. If the audience likes it, tell them it was one of your own. If they make a beeline for the restrooms, discreetly move to the next song.

Some bands never utter a word on stage because of shyness or the feeling that the music should do the talking. Although they were one of the biggest arena acts in rock, Pink Floyd spent most of their performances shoe-gazing. Maybe that's why their shows had spectacular special effects. It takes time to know the right amount of stage talk. If you have to err, do so on the side of silence; being a motor mouth when people want to hear music will not win you any popularity contests.

As obvious as it sounds, be yourself. If you're funny, great. If you're not, don't force jokes that should never see the light of day. As the song says, all you "gotta do is act naturally." No one wants to hear a phony baloney talk as if he or she is cool and everyone else is not.

Got My Eye on You, Babe

make eye contact with your audience. People most likely paid a cover charge to hear your band, deciding that you were more interesting than Brady Bunch reruns on cable. Let people know you're glad they came out to hear you by connecting with them. If looking directly at people is too distracting, try looking just above people's heads, seemingly making eye contact with the person right behind. Some musicians like to look at the back wall.

As mentioned, playing on stage can be scary. Here are some ways musicians hide or cut themselves off from the audience: constantly turning their backs to the audience, closing their eyes while singing entire songs, being mesmerized by their fret or keyboard, hiding under a large hat. Granted, it won't be fatal if a bass player does some of these things. A lead singer, however, should make a special effort to break any of these habits. The lead singer presents the song; anything that interferes with the presentation of that song has to go.

Annie Lennox, formerly of the Eurythmics, called the connection between performer and audience an "invisible bridge."[3] The task of building that bridge begins with the performer. Respect the

audience; let people in on the fun. Don't underesti-
mate listeners by giving them a half-baked effort.
They know when you are faking it and when you
are making it. You should keep in mind that the
audience might or might not want you; but you
need them. If you don't treat your fans right, there
are many other bands ready to soak up their attention. Ultimately, your audience allows you to do
the thing you enjoy doing: playing music. You
won't get asked to do so if the club's chairs are
gathering dust by your third gig.

Your Set List

Pacing your set is as important a part of
your music as the individual songs themselves. Think about the flow of your set
list. Do you want to start with a bang,
slightly mellow in the middle, then rock the rafters
at the end? Or do you want to sneak up on your
audience with a low-key beginning, then build
through the set to the big finale? Or do you want to
come on like gangbusters, then slide out of the set
with a contemplative ballad?

The following are some hints for creating a
set list:

• Avoid lining up two or three songs in the
same key or that have similar chord structures.
• If your band has more than one lead singer, try
to alternate lead vocals.

- Avoid playing songs that have the same topic in a row.
- Mix the slow songs with fast. Two ballads back-to-back may zone out your audience to the point of no return.

Using the same set list for several gigs can be comforting in its familiarity. By the same token, it is time to write up a new set list when everyone in the band has the song order memorized. Keep a number of set lists and rotate them. Write your set list in large black letters on at least an 8½" by 11" piece of paper. And have three copies on stage: one for the drummer and one for each side of the stage. A sure way to look awkward on stage is to have all players hovering over and squinting at one small piece of paper on the floor.

Give Me a Break

A break between sets provides a breather for both players and listeners. In theory, breaks last from fifteen to twenty minutes. In reality, breaks can stretch into forty minutes if someone in the band isn't watching the clock. All band members should take it upon themselves to get back on stage at the appropriate time. If this approach doesn't work, pick one person to round up players. Try to stick to a fifteen-minute break; people get restless when the break seems endless. And if the club owner says forty-five minute sets with fifteen-minute breaks, do just that if you are interested in playing the establishment again.

Playin' Makeup, Wearing Guitar

finally, what band members wear may be a key component to your stage show or not matter at all. From the heyday of rock and roll, some performers have dressed flamboyantly for performances, while others have shunned flashy duds. Little Richard sported zoot suits. Buddy Holly and the Crickets dressed like high school chemistry teachers.

In the 1970s, David Bowie, Slade, and others pioneered glam, a style in which dress, heavy gender-bending face makeup, and platform shoes were as important as the music itself. By the same token, the torn jeans and flannel shirts of Seattle's "grunge" bands were also fashion statements—or anti-statements—that advertised musical sensibilities: The loose ends were left untucked in the songs, too.

Ask yourself if what you wear on stage projects the image you wish to portray. If your band plays Bruce Springsteen-style tunes of working-class woe and you hit the stage in a fright wig and fishnets, listeners will think twice about your sincerity. Then again, the irony may draw a crowd. Just be sure that is the effect you want.

Booking

the party is history, your maiden voyage into the uncharted waters of performance complete. The show went well, all things considered. Maybe the guitar player broke three strings in four songs. Or possibly the keyboard player kicked off a song in the wrong key. But all in all, you had a blast. And so did the audience. People were listening, dancing, and enjoying themselves. Congratulations flowed like honey. All that hard work finally paid off.

Resist the temptation to rest on your laurels (or any posterior part of your anatomy). All those folks who thought your band was great are going to want to hear you again. But you can't have a party every weekend. It is time to get down to the business of booking gigs.

The entire band can think of places to play or offer leads or contacts. But one person should be in charge of booking. Several people scheduling gigs may lead to conflicting commitments. Choosing one person to handle the booking can help avoid unpleasant exchanges like "Did you call Marvin's Music Agency?" "No, I thought *you* were going to do that." Also, people who book bands like to deal with one person. When asking for a repeat gig, you as the booking person have already established a relationship with the person in charge of hiring bands.

Obviously, the person designated to book the band should have good organizational skills (not one of those who lose their wallets every time they step out the front door). When booking, schedule all performances as tentative, then check dates and times with band members to make sure everyone is available. Record all gigs, tentative or confirmed, in an appointment book. The booking person must also ask for what is easily overlooked but always essential: directions to the gig. You won't impress the music lover who hires you by showing up late, or missing your slot because you thought you knew the location of the gig.

Your ideal band representative should be both courteous *and* persistent. He or she must be easy to talk with, both in person and on the phone. A cooler-than-thou attitude may work for the stage, but can annoy clients. By the same token, the person who schedules shows should be persistent and not easily intimidated. He or she shouldn't be bothered by calling potential bosses ten times before getting them on the phone and another ten to get an answer.

If no one in your band fits this description or wants to assume the responsibility, find an outside person to do the job. Regardless of who does the booking, consider paying that person 5 to 10 percent of what the band earns. A person who proves to be a successful booker is worth the cut. Your band can be hotter than Death Valley in August, but no one will hear your scorching sound if there are no gigs on the calendar.

The Promo Pack

Say the person voted most likely to succeed at booking is you. The next step is to develop a promo, or promotional, pack to sell your band. A promo pack—also called a press kit, press package, or media kit—has four basic ingredients: the cover letter, a demo tape, a photograph, and an informational sheet about the band.

The Cover Letter

The cover letter introduces your band and states your desire to play to the person who you hope will hire you. Write to a specific person. If you address your letter to anybody at the local rock club, nobody will want to read it because it wasn't individually addressed. A phone call to your potential venue is the best way to find out whom you should contact.

In the cover letter, refer to your phone call. Jog the hiring person's memory by mentioning that he or she requested the press kit. The letter should be brief—one page—and reiterate what you said on the phone: You are a such-and-such kind of band, you have or don't have a P.A., there are four pieces in the group, and so on. Impress upon the person how much you would like to play. But don't gush. The person reading your letter will be turned off by phoniness.

Type your cover letter. Even if you aced penmanship in the sixth grade, longhand is difficult to read and looks less professional than typed text. And use good quality paper. Flimsy report paper doesn't cut it. Use heavy stock, preferably white or off-white. Do your best to make the letter mistake-free. Simple, direct sentences with correct grammar will go a long way to getting your foot inside the booking person's door. True, you are not asking to test out of English class; you are asking for a gig. But business is business. If you come across professionally in your cover letter and promo pack, the logical extension is that the band is professional and, therefore, an act the hiring person will want to book.

The Demo Tape

Not surprisingly, the demo, or demonstration, tape is the most important part of the promo pack. In the early stages of a band, it is hard to scrape together enough money to do an actual studio recording, a subject explored in more depth in Chapter Six. So what's a new group to do? Depending on its quality, record with the equipment you are using in your rehearsal sessions. For a not-so-outrageous fee, you can rent quality recording equipment from a local music store and tape a live performance. Out of an evening's worth of material, you will probably record three to five songs that are usable on a demo tape. Because that is how many you want on the tape. Most people need only a few songs to decide whether to hire a band. If you send a demo tape with fourteen songs, the hiring person will probably only listen to three. Put your best song first, second-best song second, and, well, you get the idea. Don't make the mistake of building to your strongest material. If the first song on the tape is just okay, chances are the listener will hit the eject button before the intro of the second song.

Some bands include more songs on a demo tape by recording parts of songs. This approach helps bands with a variety of sounds but also requires studio recording capability to fade from one song segment to another. If your band plays in a variety of styles, consider having a couple of demos. One might be an electric demo showcasing your hard-driving material. The second demo might highlight your acoustic set that emphasizes vocals and fine fingerwork. Keep in mind, though, the person who hires you as the easy-listening band won't appreciate it if you suddenly plug in and bring the house down.

A demo tape should be a clean, easy-to-listen-to production. If you are promoting original music, vocals and lyrics should be clear and easy to understand. Save extended jams for the stage; your demo tape songs should highlight the words, melodies, and band sound so that the booking person has a good idea of what you sound like.

Always use high-quality tape for your demos, preferably in a length that roughly matches how much music you have. Music stores sell tapes of five minutes in length and up. And don't forget to break the tabs on your master cassette so you won't accidentally record over it.

Choosing the songs to represent your band on the first demo can be a challenge. Your rhythm guitar player may want to include a song that he wrote, even if it isn't one of your band's strongest tunes, or the lead guitar player may pick a weaker song simply because he has a great solo in it. The best rule of thumb is for individual band members to tuck away their egos and decide which songs work best for the band.

The recording quality of your tape can also come into play. If you have a terrific song, but the machine went haywire and gave you a loopy recording, don't use it. If you blew your show-stopping number on recording night, leave it off. Whatever makes it on the demo has to sound good in its own right. All the songs should be recorded on one side of the tape. It may not seem like a big deal, but having to flip over a tape is often more effort than a booking person wants to make.

Finally, choose upbeat material. If you have a terrific ballad, include it. If you have two great ballads, pick one. Most people go to music clubs for the excitement of live music. If the booking person thinks your demo is a sleeping pill, you won't get the gig. Your demo tape is your calling card; make it reflect the talented band that you are.

The Photograph

A black-and-white 8" by 10" glossy is the standard photograph used in the promo pack. If you have the money, hire a professional to take your picture, preferably in a studio. It is more difficult to get an outdoor shot to look good in terms of lighting and exposure. Try different photo compositions: the head shot, with instruments, without instruments, playing, or doing something completely unrelated to music like playing cards or eating pizza. Do you want everyone laughing or looking energetic, or do you prefer the cool look? Make sure the background doesn't interfere with you as the subject. The viewer should not to have to search for you in the picture.

Some bands prefer a live shoot, a photo session while the band is playing a gig. This kind of shoot can be tough. Getting the technical elements of the photograph to jibe with a terrific picture of your band in action is a creative crapshoot. If you can make it work, great. Whether live or in the studio, shooting a group of people is tricky. You don't want your photo to look like a family portrait or a high school yearbook snap of the debating team.

Many bands shoot overly artistic photos to show their uniqueness. If this urge overcomes your band, take a collective deep breath and let it pass. Band photos with groovy effects like motion blurring, out-of-focus, incongruous proportions, and high contrast are more annoying than creative. The photograph lets the booking person know what you look like, which in the final analysis, is not all that important. It doesn't hurt if your lead singer looks like he or she just stepped off a magazine cover. But looks, no matter how stunning, will never replace musical talent. That is not to say you can't use creativity in setting up your photo shoot. Just know the difference between a photograph that is clear, direct, and imaginative and one that relies on too many effects.

If you don't have the money to hire a photographer, ask a friend with a 35mm camera to do the job. That person should shoot three to four rolls of film; it takes a lot of film to get a photograph everyone likes. Bring several things to wear to a shoot. If you wear a shirt that totally disgusts the rest of the band, it is good to have clothing options.

If you want to have a large number of promotional photographs made, certain photo developers specialize in printing glossies with the band's name, phone number, and logo in the bottom margin.

The Informational Sheet

Whoever gets A's in English should be drafted to write the informational sheet. The sheet should be just that—one page—and start with a brief description of the band. If you are primarily a dance band, say so. If you do mostly political songs, put that down. If you've had anything written about your band in a school or city paper or community newsletter (and they liked you!) include the juiciest quotes, if not the entire article. Remember, you are selling the band, so don't be shy about your talents. Likewise, don't include comments that you can't live up to. Saying you are the rockin'est band to ever shake a dance floor, then not delivering, will only backfire with the most humiliating results.

The informational sheet should also list the band members, giving short but relevant background on each person. Granted, you may not have much in your background, especially if this is your first band experience. Anything musical, from singing the lead in your junior high school's production of *West Side Story* to giving piano lessons, is fair game.

The songs on your demo tape should also be listed on the informational sheet, along with the songs' authors. The information sheet should be typed and free from spelling and grammatical errors. No one expects you to have the writing skills of a Madison Avenue advertising executive, but clarity and neatness will help convey your message.

The name of the band and phone number of the booking person should appear on all four pieces of the promo pack. If the hiring person loses three out of four pieces, he or she will still have your phone number. Dropping off promo packs in person is a good way to meet the hiring person face-to-face. When making follow-up calls, you are then not just an anonymous voice on the phone. If pressed for time, the U.S. Postal Service is a reliable way to get promo packs into the hands of your intended.

Many bands put their promo pack pieces in a folder with a pocket to hold the demo tape. You can have your band's name and logo printed on the front of the folder; be wary, however, of spending too much cash on niceties like these. Those professional touches are fine if you don't have to open a financial vein in the process. Your promo pack lives and dies on the demo. If that is strong, everything else will follow.

Where to Play?

Once you have developed your promo pack, the question of where to play arises. Most working bands play in clubs or bars that serve alcohol. Though laws vary from state to state, generally musicians under the legal drinking age can play in clubs or bars; if, however, an underage musician is caught drinking alcohol, he or she can be issued a citation for a Class C misdemeanor and asked to appear before a judge within seven to ten days. If that musician pleads guilty to the charge of being a minor in possession of or consuming alcoholic beverages, he or she can be fined several hundred dollars. If the player pleads innocent, there will be some kind of trial.

That is what happens most of the time, but it is by no means the only thing that can happen. If the arresting officer decides that you, as the minor, are acting in a manner that poses a threat to yourself or other people, that officer can escort you to the local detention area. In translation, if you are talking back, not cooperating, and generally having a bad attitude, the cop can handcuff you and haul you off to jail. The owner of the club can also be fined up to a thousand dollars for serving you a cold brew, possibly do jail time, and in some states, lose his or her liquor license for a period of time. Understandably, some club owners are reluctant to hire underage musicians; the reality is that underage musicians play regularly in bars. Call the Bureau of Alcohol, Tobacco and Firearms (which might also be called the Alcoholic Beverage Commission or the Liquor Control Board) in your state to determine whether an underage musician can play a club that serves alcohol.

That's the law. Now on to a higher authority. Your parents may not let you play in a club that serves alcohol. And they should know where you are playing. If you are still living at home, your parents have the right to nix playing in bars and clubs. Talk with your parents about this subject. Whether you can play a club that serves alcohol will depend on the club itself, your parents' attitude toward alcohol, and whether you would accept a parent in the audience as a watchdog.

Types of Venues

If you can't play Joe's Bar, don't despair. There are other places to play. Many cities have underage clubs that cater to a high-school-age clientele and do not serve alcohol. Also, many regular music clubs, especially during summertime, have teen nights. These nights are set aside exclusively for kids younger than the legal drinking age. No alcohol is served, and the cover is high enough for the club owners to pay the band and maybe part of the electric bill.

School dances are a staple of the new band, but how about playing at community center functions, the annual church bazaar, the new gas station opening? It takes ingenuity to think up new places to play, then salesmanship to convince the right person to let you do the job.

Open Mikes

Open mikes are a time-honored way for new performers to get their feet wet and for club owners to fill a slower night, usually a Sunday or Monday, with free music. Although the format varies, open mikes usually consist of performers signing up a few hours before actual playing time. Musicians play only two or three songs or are limited to a certain amount of time—usually fifteen minutes. Open mikes tend to be more successful for smaller, acoustic-type bands. Needless to say, you're not going to set up a drum kit for three songs. But if you have open mikes in your area and yours is the kind of band that could benefit from the experience, forge ahead.

New Band Nights

First cousin to the open mike is the new band night. Like open mikes, new band nights are usually held on slower nights and feature acts trying to get through those potentially awkward first-time stage jitters. Unlike open mikes, new band nights are coordinated in advance; four or so groups each play a thirty- to forty-five-minute set. Often, new band nights function as live auditions. Many booking people prefer hearing a live set to attacking the mountain of demo tapes on their desks. The live performance is what counts. You may have been able to put together a terrific demo, but if you can't play well live, keep rehearsing until you can.

Many clubs with new band nights pay the bands by the ticket system. Each band is given a stack of tickets of a certain color. Band members pass out the tickets, flattering, cajoling, and begging their friends to come out to the gig. The tickets are collected as payment at the door. At the end of the night, the management counts up the tickets, and pays the bands a nominal (very nominal) fee based on the number of tickets collected. This system also lets the management know how many people you brought in. If tickets collected show that 70 percent of the crowd was there to see your band, chances are you'll get asked to play again, maybe later in the week or on the weekend.

Benefits

Benefits are another staple of the new band. Non-profit organizations are constantly looking for free talent to play at their fund-raisers. Helping a worthy cause can give a band a sense of satisfaction. It is also a great way to gain experience and exposure. Playing benefits, however, is not a way to fill your band's coffers as most will be freebies on your part.

Each band member should feel comfortable about playing a certain benefit. Be aware that not everyone in the band will share the same political or social sensibilities. It is not worth the internal strife for a band to argue over whether to play a Pro-Choice rally. If one person in the band doesn't want to play a benefit, for whatever reason, respect that decision and let the benefit pass. Any pluses gained from playing for a crowd will be nullified by the tension among band members that will remain long after the benefit is over.

Opening Slots

If you have friends in established bands, ask if you can open for them. You have to be good enough to not embarrass your friends. Help set up and tear down the P.A. and play no longer than thirty minutes. Don't get too pushy about your involvement in the gig, and don't ask for money. Let the band know that you will do your best to get your friends out to the gig, which will help the headlining act build its audience. And don't forget, you are the opening act. If you try to grandstand, the band that was nice enough to share their gig time will never let you open for them again.

Local Access Video

Most urban areas have local access TV channels. These channels cablecast programming produced by local people who want to express their interests or opinions. Local access channels are constantly searching for new material. Call access stations to see if anyone is producing segments on local bands. Being videotaped is invaluable for a new band. Seeing what you look like while performing can be both exhilarating and instructive. Study the tape to improve your overall performance.

Being on television provides great exposure for your band. But keep in mind, a local access channel is not MTV; most of the people involved are not professionals. Nevertheless, exploring the possibilities of local access channels can lead to interesting possibilities.

Regular Gigs

The best way to get your band off the ground is to play a regular gig. If your band plays every Friday night at the local pizza restaurant, people know where to find you. True, having gigs all over town is preferable to no gigs at all. But playing the same place consistently over time is a great way to build a following. Make a note of where bands similar to yours are playing. If a band plays every Saturday night at a club or restaurant, that band might break up or get a better gig elsewhere. Be ready to jump into that prime slot by sending a promo pack to the venue.

Club owners and agents notice whether you can draw a crowd. Some hiring people are actually interested in and knowledgeable about music. But many who book are only interested in the size of the band's following. No matter what a hiring person thinks of your music, he or she will ask your band to play again if you bring in people who buy food or drinks. Likewise, you won't get a second look if you can't draw customers, even if you are the most innovative band in town. To the club, bar, or restaurant owner, the band is first and foremost a tool to increase profits—their profits, not yours.

Money, Honey

the types of gigs discussed so far—new band nights, open mikes, and others— involve little or no money. Playing for free or for pay that makes minimum wage look like a fortune has its advantages. You get paid in exposure and experience instead of cash. Still, your band has expenses. Try to balance free gigs with paid dates. If you only do freebies, you might have a hard time getting paying gigs.

Say you've garnered praise and a few fans by playing low- or no-wage gigs. You're ready to progress to better-paying jobs. But how much can you reasonably charge? It would be impossible to give actual number amounts on what you can expect to earn from gigs. Answering the following questions will help you to decide your asking price.

What is the size of the venue and how many people will you be playing for? As a general rule, you can ask for more money if the establishment or audience is large.

Is the gig a public date, meaning at a club or some event that is open to the public, or is it a private event? You can ask for more cash for private events; clubs and restaurants don't have large music budgets. Budgets for onetime events like private parties tend to be fatter. But unless you're playing a shindig for a recent lottery winner, those budgets have their limits, too.

How much does the hiring person want you to play? Three sets will cost more than one for obvious reasons. Do you have to drive a distance to get to the gig? Travel will also increase the price.

Will you have to set up your own P.A. or rent a system? If you can play acoustically, no P.A. means less time and hassle for the band, which translates to less expenditure for the hiring person.

Suppose you've played a gig that had a considerable paycheck. How will you divide your financial rewards? If you are in a democratic-type band, the split should be equal among band members. If you are in a leader-type band, the name up front will get a bigger piece of the pie. Problems arise when a member in the first type of band wants more money than the others. Your band's name will help to decide how to divide the money: If you are Joe and the Shmoes, Joe gets a bigger cut. If you are the Shmoes, everyone gets an equal cut, no matter if you have a Joe who thinks his presence is worth more.

Playing in a band is fun work. It is rarely, however, an activity that brings in vast sums of money—at least on the local level. When you *do* make money, the temptation is to blow it on a new pair of high-tops. Even though the new shoes might look cool on stage, think about reinvesting your hard-earned cash back into the band. Every band has expenses for equipment that needs to be bought or repaired, promotion overhead, payback on the P.A. loan, and so on. Try not to expect that your band earnings will finance a spring break trip to the beach.

Let's Make a Deal

So how *can* you get the best deal for your band? Negotiating with a club owner or booking agent takes practice. Here is a list of tips for making the initial business negotiations, usually done when you call to book your gig.

> Call at a good time. If you're contacting a restaurant with a booming lunch business, don't call at noon. Be persistent in your calling but don't annoy by being unaware of the hiring person's situation.
>
> Be courteous to everyone, not only to potential bosses. You may think the person answering the phone is just a waiter, but he may be the owner's son. Regardless of whether that person is the owner's son or not, treat everyone

with respect. On a business level it makes sense because today's waiter is tomorrow's club owner. On a human level, everyone wants to be treated with dignity.

Be prepared. Find out as much as you can in advance about the establishment and the booking person. Is the person hot-tempered, slow to make decisions, rude, friendly? Knowing more about who is on the other end of the line will make the initial call less nerve-racking.

Ask yourself why this person should hire you. Then prepare yourself to answer the question. You are an easy band to work with. You play the kind of music that is appropriate for the venue. You draw a good crowd or have the potential to do so, and so on. Practice tooting your own horn in a relaxed way so you come across as a confident professional, not an egotistical maniac.

Don't slam the receiver after the person says he or she is not interested in booking your band. Club owners share their experiences with other booking people. If you lose your cool, it will hurt your chances of getting future work. Fortunately, the converse is true. If you realize that negotiations are not personal and you stay professional throughout the making of a deal, word of your professionalism will spread.

If the club owner calls and you aren't in a situation where you can talk, ask to return the call later. Negotiating takes focus; if you can't concentrate because final exams start the next day, ask to call back at another time.

Sign on the Dotted Line

the issue of whether you need a written contract comes up while negotiating gigs. Yes, a written contract is a good way for both parties to see on paper what has been discussed and decided on. The truth is that most local club owners don't use written contracts, not because they are dishonest (although some are) but because written contracts are a bother. A verbal agreement is usually enough to make a local deal happen. A written contract, however, is essential for an out-of-town gig. The contract should state the terms agreed upon and be signed by both parties. A written contract is simply a business tool; the hiring person who is insulted by your request for one is to be avoided at all costs.

If the club owner or booking agent gives you a contract to sign, read it over with eagle eyes. Question anything you don't understand. Asking questions doesn't make you seem dumb. It shows that you are smart enough to know when something is not clear and confident enough to get the information you need in order to make good business decisions.

The music business involves both music and business. Negotiating the business of being in a band is a job in itself. Many terrific bands have gone down the tubes because of inept business practices. Ultimately, making a deal should be a win-win situation. While both parties might not get exactly what they want, they should feel satisfied with the transaction. For a more in-depth look at the art and skill of negotiating, read Bob Woolf's *Friendly Persuasion*. This easy-to-read book is filled with useful information on how to make a deal, and much of the advice reaches beyond the limits of the business world.

Bookkeeping

along with the job of booking gigs, another nonmusical task is that of managing the band's finances. If the band had to take a loan from United Bank of Your Parents to buy the P.A., records should be kept of the payment schedule. Photographs and postage—as well as T-shirts, mailing lists, posters, and other topics to be discussed later—need to be paid for by the band.

Elect one person to take care of money matters. That person should record in a notebook or ledger how much money is earned from what gigs and how much is spent on what purchases. Whether or not you are living at home, you need to file a Schedule C, self-employed business return if you as an individual earn more than a certain amount (in 1994 it was $600) from the band. Keep receipts from purchases that are band-related and accurate mileage records for driving to and from gigs. Deductions are the tax-paying musician's friend. Don't pay more in taxes than you have to.

Spread the Word

the calendar is slowly filling up with gigs, maybe less than you'd hoped for, but more than your worst fear—none. Now you should concentrate on letting the public know where you are playing. If the venue will spring for an ad in the local paper, so much the better. But you can do a lot to promote your gigs, through flyers and posters, a mailing list, local listings, and T-shirt sales.

Flyers and Posters

An eye-catching flyer will let people know where you are playing. If you've never made a flyer before, the staff at your local copy shop will answer your questions. Most flyers are on 8½" by 11" or 11" by 14" sheets of paper. Copy shops have a variety of colored papers; electric colors work best to make your flyer stand out.

Posters are basically flyers with class. If you have a computer, print out when and where your band is playing, using different sizes and fonts. Or a band member with artistic skill can do some interesting (but readable) lettering. Posters can feature black-and-white drawings, again done by a person with artistic talent. You can also use clip art, small black-and-white drawings that come in a variety of styles and on various subjects. Or use your promo photos to give your poster a professional look. If you are using a photograph, ask the copy shop to reproduce your test poster on the photo setting. Not all copy machines reproduce photos well, but those with a photo setting do a good job.

You can make a more expensive generic poster on which you handwrite gig information, then photocopy. If you decide to make a more expensive poster with a photograph, you can use the negative.

No matter what format you choose, posters and flyers are an inexpensive way to get the word out about your band. Put up your posters and flyers wherever they are allowed. If you put them up where they are not wanted, they will end up in the trash. If you are in a store, community center, or anywhere else, ask before you get out your thumb tacks or tape. And don't put your poster or flyer over someone else's advertisement. Competition between bands is fine, even good if it motivates the bands to do their best. But every band should have a chance to get its message to the public.

Mailing List

Another good promotional device is the mailing list. At each gig, leave a clipboard with paper and a pen at a convenient location so people can write down their names and addresses. Mention your mailing list on stage. Then send fans notice of where you are playing for an individual gig or for a month or even a couple of months of gigs. The people who receive your calendar are being reminded of the band's name; if they liked your music enough to put their names on your mailing list, eventually they will come to hear you again. And maybe they'll bring their friends!

The downside to the mailing list is the cost of postage. Every band wants a mailing list that is a mile long, but paying regular postage adds up. Many bands put their calendars on postcards (your copy shop can show you how to do this), which makes them cheaper to mail. If you have a substantial mailing list, think about using the third-class rate or bulk mail. In order to qualify for bulk mail rates, you have to have over a certain amount of mail pieces, pay an annual fee, and comply with bulk mailing rules. If you are mailing out 500 pieces eight or nine times a year, the saving is worth the hassle of bulk mailing. If you have only 200 pieces, the cost break is not enough to justify a bulk mailout. Local bands with longevity can have mailing lists into the thousands. Bulk mail is a necessity for them. Weigh the pros and cons to see if bulk mail is for your band.

Stop the Presses

get to know local music journalists. Send your band's calendar to those writers, inviting them out to gigs. Editorial coverage—reviews of recordings or live shows (assuming it is fairly positive)—can pump new life into a band. And it's free publicity, to boot. Find out which local papers have music listings for club dates. Generally local club listings are free for the band or venue. Get your gig information in on time. Newspapers live by deadlines; if you miss those deadlines, your information won't make it into the listings.

For bigger gigs, such as a CD release party or a special onetime event, send a press release to local music writers. A press release is a letter stating the who, what, when, where, and why of your event. Any format that includes this information is acceptable. Keep it brief (writers get bags of press releases), and be sure to include a phone number in case you forgot some crucial detail or the journalist wants to do a half-page spread on your band for the Sunday edition.

T-Shirts

Another promotional activity involves the selling of band shirts at gigs. T-shirts promote the band itself as opposed to individual gigs. And while it is fun to wear a shirt with your band's name plastered all over it, it's even more exciting to see someone else wearing your shirt in the grocery store. As with the poster, find someone whose artwork you like and ask or hire that person to draw a design. After all band members agree on a drawing that includes the name of your band, look in the Yellow Pages under T-shirts/Retail. Get prices from different companies, then pick one you can afford. The company will make a film positive—a black rendition on clear film—from the artwork. Then it will print the art from the film positive onto the T-shirts. A few tips for a better T-shirt: Thin lines on the original drawing won't print well, and a simple design generally works better than a complex one.

Consider how much money you have to spend on your T-shirts. Your least expensive option is to print black ink on a white shirt made of cotton and polyester. Other colors or 100 percent cotton shirts will add to the cost.

T-shirts are printed in increments of 12, the most effective cost quantity being a gross, or 144 shirts. How many T-shirts you want depends on how many you think you can sell. If your band is setting the world on fire, 144 T-shirts may not be enough. Even though you don't have a crystal ball, try to determine how many T-shirts you can reasonably unload. If you get too many, they will end up in someone's closet instead of earning money to pay back on the original investment.

Logo

A logo is a picture that represents your band. It can be just an image like the Rolling Stones' tongue, or a stylized version of the band's name. Think of familiar band logos, like the Grateful Dead's skull and roses. A logo should reflect the image and attitude of the band. Picking a logo is like choosing a name; it might take time and discussion to come to a final decision. A logo is a great way for people to identify your band. Some bands make rubber stamps of their logos to stamp them where appropriate. Use your logo on posters, T-shirts, mailing lists, and press releases.

Business Card

You can also use your logo on a business card. If someone wants to hire your band for a party, you should whip out your business card and say you'd be delighted to play. Scrounging around for a scrap of paper on which to write your band's number is definitely unprofessional.

Generally, the smallest run of business cards is 500. Printed in black and white with two main lines and a name and address, they will cost around $20. The cost can reach around $40 if the card has colored paper and inks or more lines of text. Most copy shops do business cards; if you want your logo on your business card, the shop can reduce the image to the correct size. The card should have on it the band's name, one or two phone numbers, and a comment that will refresh the reader's memory about your band. If hiring persons find your card in their pockets two months after your meeting, a brief phrase about what you do will jog their memory. The salesperson at the copy shop will help you pick a font, choose card stock and color, and lay out the card. Be sure to spell everything correctly; the copy shop will typeset exactly what you have written, even if it is obvious to you that it is a mistake.

The card is another place you can stretch yourself creatively. Artwork or reverse printing such as white-on-black or black-on-gold are different ways to enhance your card.

Guest Lists

Allowing a limited number of people to attend your gigs at no charge can also be a good promotional strategy. Radio DJs, music journalists, booking agents, or club owners should be considered first as candidates for your guest list, followed by only the one person (two at the most) closest to each band member. Many clubs allow no more than two guests per band member, not counting industry pros. But if that's not the case, consider making this maximum a band rule. Inviting the entire senior class may pack the house; it also makes for slim returns in pay. Your friends should understand that a band is an expensive ship to keep afloat and be willing to help you out by paying their own way. To avoid awkward situations, don't hang around the front door as people come in. Friends won't be tempted to ask you to get them in free if you're not in the area.

Advancing the Gig

You've spread your promo packs all over town, made follow-up calls, and stayed cool when the booking person told you for the fifth time to call back in a week because he or she hasn't gotten to your tape yet. And guess what? It's paid off. That sixth time you called, lo and behold, the booking person has a Thursday night with your name on it. So what do you do after you've called your bandmates and collectively bounced off the walls from ecstasy? You need to advance the gig.

Advancing the gig means calling the club to confirm the booking a week or so before the date. People who book are human, and humans make mistakes. Maybe the hiring person double booked, meaning he or she inadvertently promised the same night to two bands. Or maybe you got your signals crossed: The hiring person put you down for the first Friday of the month, and you heard the last Friday. The ways in which people miscommunicate are legion. A pre-gig phone call exposes snafus, giving enough time to fix anything that is fixable.

Another important part to advancing the gig is informing the sound person of your technical needs. Even if you bring your own P.A., the sound person will want to know as much as possible about you as a band. Give the sound person a technical rider, a piece of paper describing your band's electrical needs. Then, when you show up for the gig, that sound person already knows how many people are in the band, what instruments they play, how many vocal mikes are needed, and so on. You can also draw up what is called a stage plot, a bird's-eye view of your band on stage. The stage plot shows where the players are on stage, what they play, who sings, who doesn't, and so on. It is a useful way for the sound person to keep track of what is happening on stage. Remember, the sound person mixes many different kinds of bands. Anything that helps that person mix your band is worth the effort.

Showing up at a gig with some kind of special technical need that sends the sound person into a snit is bad for everyone. Perhaps the sound person could have accommodated you had he or she known to bring that certain piece of equipment. A sound person who is annoyed has less ability to focus on mixing you to your best advantage. Be kind to sound people. They are in a no-win situation—when the sound stinks, the sound per-

Stage Plot

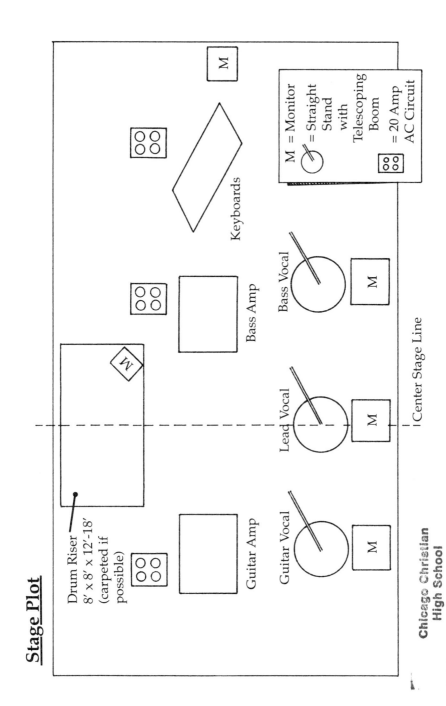

Drum Riser
8' x 8' x 12'-18'
(carpeted if possible)

Guitar Amp

Guitar Vocal

Bass Amp

Bass Vocal

Keyboards

Lead Vocal

M

M

M

M

M

Center Stage Line

M = Monitor

= Straight Stand with Telescoping Boom

= 20 Amp AC Circuit

Chicago Christian
High School

MEDIA CENTER

son is verbally hung by the thumbs, regardless of what equipment or situations they have to deal with. When the sound is great, hey, they're a killer band, aren't they?

Testing, One, Two, Three . . .

If possible, do a sound check before every gig. A sound check means setting up and testing the P.A. several hours before actual playing time. Sound people go gray watching a band roll in fifteen minutes before starting time to sound check or set up their P.A. Setting up a modest-sized P.A. with a sound check takes an hour or more. By setting up the P.A. in advance, you and the sound person can catch the little things that go wrong but are fixable: battery changes for instruments or effects boxes, busted cords, dead strings, and so on. Avoid hauling speakers and setting levels while your audience is filtering in. The best approach is to have everything set up well before the patrons arrive. A sound check insures that your first couple of songs won't be throwaways.

Road Gigs

Look for out-of-town work after you have established yourself in your hometown. Trying to build an out-of-town audience without a strong hometown following is like building a house on sand. Your local following is your foundation. Make sure it is strong before you venture out for gigs.

If you are ready to play beyond your city limits, it is imperative that you advance the gig. Driving four hours only to find out that there is no gig is tough on band morale. Coordinate travel plans and accommodations in advance. Make sure your vehicle is roadworthy. The frustration factor can go through the roof if you, your instruments, and your P.A. have to hitchhike the last 10 miles (16 kilometers) to the gig. Pick up a local map of the city or town you are going to, if at all possible. Allow enough time to drive to the gig, set up, and have dinner. Don't put the pedal to the metal because you allowed three hours for a four-hour trip.

A place to stay is sometimes part of the deal struck by you and the out-of-town club owner, but not always. If your band plans to stay with an old friend of the guitarist, make sure the guitarist calls that friend to see if four people can crash in his or her living room. If no free overnight accommodations are available, make a reservation in advance at an inexpensive motel, preferably near the gig.

One more aspect about playing out-of-town. Chapter Six deals with the making of a cassette or CD; playing dates in nearby cities and towns will be more productive if the band has a recording to sell. Leaving behind your music in the form of cassettes or CDs will remind fans of your existence. Your band will more likely fall into the "out of sight, out of mind" category if you don't have a recording to promote at out-of-town gigs.

chapter six

Studio Madness:
The Recording Experience

Sonny, is it dumb enough?[1]

What I do is almost psychodynamics. You've got to be indirect, create a diversion, trick the artist into giving something he doesn't want to give. Something extra, magic — his soul, dammit. Good production borders on the criminal.[2]

The first comment was made by Phil Spector to Sonny Bono, the second by Jim Dickinson. Both Spector and Dickinson have been called studio wizards, producers whose skill consists of taking tunes in their unrefined state and turning them into the finished—and sometimes brilliant— songs that pour from your speakers. Both comments illustrate the extremes of the recording process: the ridiculous and the near-spiritual.

Prepare yourself for those two extremes if your band is considering entering the studio. And if you've been playing regular gigs, you should think about recording. Chances are those people who have been showing up at your gigs will want a cassette or CD of your music.

Side A, Side B

before you look for a recording studio, choose the songs you want on your tape or CD. As with picking songs for the demo, decide what material works best as a band. If you plan to cover another performer's song, contact the publisher of the song to get permission to record. Song publishers are listed on the tapes and CDs on which the song is recorded; if that information is not available, call BMI (Broadcast Music Incorporated) or ASCAP (the American Society of Composers, Authors and Publishers). These two companies are performing rights societies that keep track of when music is played on radio or television and pay royalties to artists. If the song you want to cover has been played on the radio, BMI or ASCAP can tell you the publishing company. Contact the publishers and follow their instructions in order to legally cover the song.

If your band decides to record original material, obtain a copyright for each song. Copyrighting proves you wrote the material; stealing songs doesn't happen often, less than the beginning songwriter would think. Still, it's a good idea to copyright your original material. To do so, contact the Library of Congress, Copyright Office, in Washington, D.C., which will send you the forms you need.

Dough Re Mi

Making a cassette or CD is a major step for any band; for a new band, the first recording is a landmark. The journey that starts with the desire to record and ends with selling the finished tape or CD from the stage or in local music stores can be strenuous. A fundamental step in that journey is finding the money to pay for the project.

Even if you save a bundle by recording at someone's free home studio, you'll still need money to make a cassette or CD. Because recording and packaging costs vary, it is difficult to say how much the project will cost. As a rule, count on spending at least $2,000 to $4,000, less if you record with your own equipment and more if you record in a studio or want your recording on CD. Given those figures, a good question follows: Where's the money going to come from?

If you are still living at home, talk with your parents about a loan, if they have that kind of cash available. Many new bands try the investment method, in effect issuing stock in the future tape. If twenty friends, parents, and relatives give you $100 each, you have $2,000. After the recording has been made, the band pays back investors with the money earned from sales, giving each investor a cassette or CD as interest. The investment approach requires intensive bookkeeping; it also hinges on how well your product sells. If it doesn't, not only will you have a large box of tapes or CDs in your closet, but you will have to deal with disgruntled investors.

Many new bands attract benefactors, people who like the music and have some money to play with. These benefactors invest in a recording and often say they don't want to interfere with the music. But if you get into a band/benefactor relationship, make sure that everyone has the same expectations.

Is the benefactor strictly a money person, or will he or she be allowed to have input into the production? What if the recording doesn't meet the benefactor's expectations? What about the payback schedule? Be sure you have answers to these questions, lest your dream investor turn into a nightmare.

Which Studio?

You've gotten the money together for the recording, hopefully without holding up the local bank or fencing the family TV. The next step is to find a studio. Many great tapes have been made in someone's home or garage studio. Using a home studio can be an affordable way to record, especially if the engineer of that studio is experienced.

If you want and can afford a more professional studio, check out the Yellow Pages under Music/Recording Studios. Call local studios and ask for the price per hour. Studios can range in cost from $10 to $75 an hour and up, depending on the experience of the engineer, the kind of equipment in the studio, what part of the country a studio is in, and other factors. Most bands that are new to the recording process want to know how much it will cost to record a certain number of songs. That question is difficult for an engineer to answer because he or she doesn't know the band, how well they know the material, how cooperative they will be in the studio, and so on. Most times the engineer will give some kind of estimate, mostly to allay the band's frustration. When you receive your estimate, keep in mind that it is only an estimate.

If you live in a small town that doesn't have a local recording studio, use the money you would have spent on studio time to rent or buy home recording equipment. Or find a recording studio in a nearby city or town and consider commuting for a couple of weekends.

Many studios specialize in certain kinds of music. The only way to find the best studio for your band and bank account is to do some detective work.

Call studios and talk with engineers. Ask about fees, equipment, and recording clientele. Ask other bands about their recording experiences. Music stores or the local musicians' union might also be able to give you information on recording studios.

When you think you have found a studio, visit the premises and talk with the engineer. Check out the place with a critical eye:

Is the control room large enough to have your entire band comfortably listen to playback? Do you respect the skill of and do you like the personality of the engineer?

Tensions can run high during the recording process; an experienced engineer can ease a new band through difficult times.

Live or Studio?

another decision to make is whether to record live or in the studio. Most studios offer the option of remote recording, meaning recording a live performance at a local club or event. Because it takes less time, a live tape is usually less expensive than a studio recording. Capturing the excitement and energy of a performance is the plus of live recording. The downside is that most live performances are not note perfect. In a live performance, the audience hears each song once; with a tape, those same songs are laid bare to the scrutiny of repeated listenings. You can record live on multiple tracks, then fix mistakes in the studio, but your costs will be comparable to that of a studio recording.

Another chancy thing about recording live is that every player may not be at his or her peak on recording day. If you choose to record live during ragweed season, your allergic vocalist may not turn in the performance of a lifetime. Or maybe the keyboard player jammed a finger during last Sunday's volleyball game. It is a gamble to record live. How confident the musicians feel, the kind of music played, and the size of the money pot bank-rolling the project are all factors in deciding whether to record live or in the studio.

What's in a Studio?

Whether a state-of-the-art setup or someone's converted garage, all studios are basically the same. The recording equipment in a studio is, not surprisingly, much like that of the P.A. In the control room, there is a mixing board that takes the signals from the line inputs from the mikes and electric instruments, adjusts for tone and volume, then sends the signal to the recording machine, be it a reel-to-reel, cassette, or DAT machine. (DAT stands for digital audiotape and is a relatively new technology that became part of the recording process in the early 1990s.) The control room also has speakers for playback and, depending on the studio, different effects machines like reverb and compressors.

A compressor narrows the dynamic range of the sound. If the recording signal is too weak, tape hiss will be audible. If it is too strong, the sound will distort. A compressor limits the range of sound by bringing down the parts that are too loud and bringing up the parts that are too quiet. You still retain a dynamic range in your music; the compressor, however, gives the ability to get as hot a signal as possible without distortion or as soft a sound as possible and still be heard.

Musicians communicate with the engineer in the control room visually through a glass panel or window and audibly through the headphones. Musicians hear live playing or prerecorded tracks through the headphones; they also talk and listen to the engineer through the mike/headphone monitor system.

Studio

Window

Studio Monitors
Controlled from
Mixing Console

Near Field Monitors

Mixing Board

Multi Track
Tape Recorder

Engineer

Vocal Mike

Headphones

DI

Headphone Connector

The headphone mix is a crucial aspect of the recording process; time should be taken to get it right. When trying to get the best mix in the headphones, be specific in your comments. Is the guitar distorted, thin, booming? Just saying it sounds bad won't help the engineer. Again, be aware of the "more me" syndrome. As with the P.A. mix on stage, the headphone mix for recording can escalate into a competition to see who gets the most volume. The recording process is a good place to draw upon all those cooperation skills your band has been honing since the first rehearsal.

Head-On Recording

there are two basic ways of recording: head-on and layering tracks. A head-on recording consists of all band members playing at the same time, essentially a live performance in a studio setting. If everyone is in one room, movable walls are put in between players to help isolate each musician's sound. This baffling makes the mixing process easier as there is less leakage from one track to another.

The head-on approach has many advantages. It is a relatively fast process, assuming you don't play each song twenty times. In the studio, time is money. If you take less time to record, less cash will flow from your pockets. For many new bands, capturing the excitement of the music while layering tracks can be difficult. Playing head-on assures that live energy, but can also mean mistakes to fix, meaning more money, or not fix, meaning living with a flawed recording.

If you decide to record head-on, do your homework. Record the songs with your home equipment, making sure you are happy with the arrangements and overall sound. Nothing is more depressing than discovering in the studio that the songs are actually riddled with mistakes. Even if you think the songs are perfect, record them and double-check harmonies, chord structure, rhythm, and so on. Nitpick to the point where the songs start to invade your dreams. You'll be glad you did when you hit the studio.

Type or neatly write out lyric sheets for the engineer to follow the songs. You may know the songs backward and forward, but most times the engineer is hearing them for the first time as they are in the process of being recorded.

Layering Tracks

In order to understand the process of layering tracks, you should first understand the nature of a multitrack recording system. A multitrack system is a series of separate yet connected recordings. Multitrack systems come in increments of eight tracks, the most common being the 8-, 16-, and 24-track systems. The more high-tech studios have 64 tracks and up, but unless your favorite uncle happens to be a recording executive in Los Angeles or New York, you probably won't get the chance to record on that kind of system.

In layering tracks, the musicians first record a rhythm track, usually guitar, bass, drums, and possibly keyboards, on a certain number of tracks, depending on the total number available. Often the vocalist sings a "scratch" or throwaway track to help the rhythm players keep their place in the song. On the next group of tracks, the lead players, both vocalist and lead instrumentalists lay down, or overdub, their tracks while listening to the playback of the rhythm track in the headphones. Harmony singers or any added instrumental embellishments are added on the remaining tracks.

With both the head-on or layered approach, musicians can fix mistakes on tracks that they otherwise want to keep. This fixing, or "punching in," means the player listens to the playback while the engineer drops out the offending part and engages the recording mode that will capture the flawless new version of the flubbed lick or line. During the actual recording process, the musician might hear a "click" as the punch is happening; on the finished product, the editing will (or should) be seamless.

Whether you record head-on, layer tracks, or use a combination, make sure you begin each recording session with all of your equipment in top working order. Having your groove interrupted by a dead 9-volt battery on a guitar effect, or a broken string that doesn't have a replacement, takes the fun out of recording. If your bass has been intermittently shorting out, get it fixed before you record. Don't gamble that the problem won't raise its ugly head during the recording process. Murphy's Law tends to rule in the studio. Do your best to keep those hair-tearing annoyances at a minimum.

The Producer

the producer is the person who oversees the recording project. That person makes the final decision about the studio, what songs to record, and their instrumentation and arrangements, among other things. The producer also gives feedback on which tracks are keepers and which need to be done over. Most new bands produce their first recording themselves, mostly because an experienced producer is not available or affordable. In the studio equation, though, problems equal time, and time equals money, so problems equal money. Though an expense, having a producer might be a band's best defense against the recording experience turning into a black hole that sucks up any cash wandering into its gravitational field.

The decision on whether to hire a producer will also depend on the dynamics of the band. Some bands need an outside person to referee; others are more comfortable with decision-making by consensus. If you know a person whose musicianship you respect and who has studio experience, consider hiring that person to produce your recording. The band/producer relationship can abound with creativity if both parties stay open to the possibilities.

Mixing and Mastering

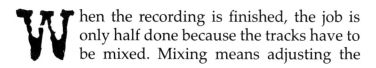

When the recording is finished, the job is only half done because the tracks have to be mixed. Mixing means adjusting the tracks for volume and tone so that the song sounds like a cohesive unit. There are as many approaches to mixing as there are musicians who record. One band may want the lead vocalist up front, with the harmony singers in the background. Another band may like the harmony singers to be as loud as the lead vocalist. Still other bands may want a "heavy" rhythm sound, pumping up the bass and drums. Whatever your approach, the mixing process is an important step in forging the studio sound of your band.

When you record and mix, watch for danger signals. Don't leave mistakes in the recording thinking you can fix everything in the mix. Some things can be fixed in the mix, but it's best to make basic tracks as error-free as possible. Mixing is a deceptively difficult process; the more integrity basic tracks have, the easier that process will be.

Yet again, the "more me" syndrome can surface in the mixing process. No one wants to record, then feel cheated in the mix. If band members can't decide on a mixing strategy, consider handing over the tapes to someone with production and mixing experience. It may be the only way to get a good product without the band exploding under the stress.

How long it will take to mix your cuts depends on a variety of things. In an expensive studio, the standard ratio of mixing to music time is sixty to one, meaning sixty minutes of mix time for every minute of recorded music. New bands who are usually financially less endowed should expect to lower that ratio significantly. Don't fall into the trap that snares many new bands, namely spending all your cash on the recording and leaving only spare change for the mix. If your band has standard instrumentation, the mix will take less time. If, however, your band plays a variety of instruments, or the same instruments are played by different band members, the mix will take longer.

Once the basic mix is done, take a few days off from listening to the tape. Then listen to the rough mix on your car stereo, home stereo, or boombox, to hear the tape on different systems. Have friends or family listen to the tape and ask for honest feedback. But don't stack the deck by saying, "I think the drums are too loud, but tell me what you think." Your friends and family don't have to be music experts to notice things that are awry. If they all say, "Gee, doesn't the guitar sound a little funny?" it's time to hit the studio and either re-record or remix.

After mixing, a final process called mastering is done. Mastering is the final mix that makes the highs and lows more cohesive from song to song. Your mastered mix won't have peaks that prick up dogs' ears or a bass range that disappears into oblivion.

Cover Art and Title

Your band has made it through the recording, mixing, and mastering of your project with hearts and minds still intact. Now it is time to think about your cover art. Take the amount of time you spent thinking about your promo photo, poster, or band logo and multiply it by ten when thinking about your cover art. Many design considerations arise. Will you use your promo photo or logo for the cover of your recording? Does the photo or art fit the dimensions of the product? How will your square band shot fit on a rectangular tape box? What will you do with the space above and below your oblong logo on your square CD? Where will you put your band's name and the recording title?

Covers of rock albums, CDs, and tapes are an art form unto themselves. Roger Dean created fantasy scenes for records by the band Yes. The photos on Aerosmith's *Pump* and *Get a Grip* may have been unsubtly suggestive, but they were also distinctive and eye-catching. While your taste may compare to Aerosmith's, your budget most probably will not.

Consider how many colors you can afford to print. Black-and-white art is the cheapest to reproduce. Two- and four-color art are more expensive. Being imaginative in creating your cover art can be fun; being imaginative on a budget can be a real challenge.

What will be the title of your recording? Many bands self-title their first recording as a way of introducing the band and recording to the world. If that doesn't thrill you, consider choosing a song title for your recording title, or maybe a key phrase from one of the songs. How about some word or phrase that relates to the recording as a whole? In general, simple or shorter titles work best. But pick a title that everyone in the band likes. If your band knows in its collective soul that your first recording must be entitled *Antidisestablishmentarianism*, go for it.

Duplication

Y ou've got your dynamite cover art and master tape of equally dynamite songs. What's next? You need copies of both, so you will have to find a duplication house. A duplication house takes your master, art, and text for the J card or CD insert, and produces your tapes or CDs. The J card is the paper inside the cassette box that contains information about the songs and recording.

To find a duplication house, ask your engineer for recommendations or consult the Yellow Pages listings under Recording Services. Once again, shop around for the best prices. A mail-order duplication house prices 300 cassettes with the printing of the cassette and J card and a black-and-white cover, with shrink wrap, between $555 and $615, depending on the quality of tape used in duplication. A 500 run of CDs with the same guidelines will run approximately $2000. Obviously there is a big difference in cost between cassettes and CDs, but you get what you pay for. CDs sound better, are more prestigious, and are likely to remain the format of choice among consumers and radio stations for some time to come. Tapes, however, are a respectable and, for a new band, affordable way to make your music available, which is the point of recording in the first place.

Recording Release Party

they're here! The whole band is staring into a large box filled with your newly minted cassettes or CDs. You should feel proud of your accomplishment; not all bands are musically or financially capable of making a recording. But you might also feel a touch of dread. That's a lot of product to sell. The best place to start is at your tape or CD release party. A release party is a combination of two things: a marketing tool to let the public know you have a cassette or CD, and a party—a time to get together with friends and fans to celebrate the arrival of the recording.

Inform local music writers of your new recording by sending them a press release. Most, though not all, release parties are at a venue that the band has been playing regularly. If you normally charge a cover at that venue, consider making the record release a free event. People can put the money they would have spent on a cover toward the purchase of the tape or CD. A free recording release party might also encourage people who are curious about your band but who don't want to invest cash in that interest. Many bands encourage the party atmosphere by bringing munchies if selling food is not a goal of the venue. Also, the band can invite other performers to play, adding to the special quality of the evening. Remember: It's your party and you can do what you want to.

chapter seven

Player Beware: Dangers in the Music World

I went to rehab 14 times. I was in pajamas for almost 14 months out of my life. And people talk about knowing drugs and knowing addiction and their belief why Kurt Cobain killed himself or why the guy from the Byrds died of alcoholism or why the guy from the Gin Blossoms killed himself or why any of the other people do the things they do.

You know what it is? It's just not having the ability to be intimate with yourself, being afraid *of that.*[1]

These are the words of Megadeth's Dave Mustaine. Three months after Nirvana's Kurt Cobain committed suicide in 1994, Mustaine was part of a group of musicians gathered by *Option* magazine to talk about depression and drug addiction, from which Cobain suffered.

Alcoholism and drug addiction—neither of these diseases recognize occupation, social standing, or age. They occur in every part of society. Yet

in rock, alcoholism and drug addiction partic-
ularly seem to be dangers that go with the job. Part
of being in a band is deciding how you will deal
with these issues and others that aren't directly
related to music or business, but matter more than
both, since in some instances they may put your
life at stake.

Drugs and Alcohol

usic, drugs, and alcohol have been
keeping company since the beginning
of popular music. Why is this so? Some
answers include too much fame and money too
soon for young musicians, the rebellious attitude
of rock, the painkilling or energy-inducing effects
of certain drugs. Even if you've been playing in a
band for only a short time, you don't have to be a
rocket scientist to recognize some patterns of drug
use. Some musicians get high because they think it
helps them with stage fright; others say they play
better stoned. Still others feel they have to live
what they *think* is the hard rockin' lifestyle, which
includes destroying themselves with both legal
and illegal substances.

The reality is that there are no good reasons to
do drugs or drink to excess before you play. Being
wasted doesn't get rid of stage fright, it just delays
dealing with it. The player who gets high to calm
performance nerves usually ends up with two
problems, stage fright and drug addiction. If you
think you can only play high, take a hard listen to
yourself playing straight. You might be pleasantly
surprised to find you play just as well straight—if

not better. And if you don't, it is time to go back to square one and start practicing.

For every musician who went to an early grave believing toxins made him or her rock harder, there are many other players who are living proof that you can be clean and produce your best work. A prime example is Aerosmith. During the mid-1970s, they were perhaps America's most popular rock band. Lead singer Steven Tyler admitted: "Our story is that basically we had it all and then we threw it all away. I snorted my airplane. I snorted my Porsche. I snorted my house."[2] The band straightened up in the late 1980s and went on to produce its strongest and most successful work.

Drugs and alcohol have an undeserved status in rock and roll. Don't fall victim to the notion that these substances somehow make you legitimate. Your music makes you legitimate. If that is not enough, maybe you should rethink why you want to be in a rock band.

Sex

drugs can work double duty when it comes to ruining your life. Not only can they destroy your body, they can impair your ability to make smart decisions. If you decide to have sex and fail to follow safer sex guidelines, your moment of passion could end in a variety of consequences. HIV and AIDS are facts of life in music, yet they have been given pitifully little attention in the rock press. Journalists and musicians seem to have agreed to follow a "don't ask, don't tell" policy. The loss to AIDS of such stars as B-52's guitarist Ricky Wilson and Queen singer Freddie Mercury has raised some awareness. By many accounts, however, the music industry as a whole has tried to avoid the topic. For a business in which many still live by the "sex, drugs, and rock and roll" motto, such silence can be deadly indeed.

Does this mean your life has to be G-rated? No. When deciding whether or not to be sexually active, have both feet planted firmly in reality. Educate yourself about safer sex and the consequences of unsafe sex and of sharing needles. Those consequences will have a direct impact on your ability to make the music that drew you into this world in the first place.

Hearing Loss

Part of rock and roll's glory is its noisiness. Many fans feel that rock music just doesn't rock if it isn't turned up to ear-splitting volume. But it shouldn't be so loud as to create hearing damage for both player and listener. If your idea of someone with hearing loss is Gramps with an ear horn, think again. Hearing loss is a real threat that affects anyone who is exposed to high-volume noise over a period of time.

When a sound wave enters the ear, it hits the eardrum and vibrates it, moving three small bones called the ossicles. As the last ossicle moves, it displaces the fluid in the inner ear, in turn stimulating hair cells also in the inner ear. Those hair cells send the bioelectric signal through the auditory nerve to the brain, which interprets the signal as the specific sound.

If the ear is repeatedly bombarded with loud sound, the sound waves overstimulate the workings of the inner ear, eventually damaging the hair cells that transmit the signal to the auditory nerve. When the auditory nerve sends only a partial signal, the brain has less information to process, translating into an inability to understand certain sounds. Unlike the hair on your head, these hair cells do not grow back or repair themselves once damaged.

The hair cells in your inner ear are frequency specific; certain hair cells interpret high-frequency sound, some mid-range, and some the low-frequency range. High-volume sound damages high-frequency hair cells first. Unfortunately, much of our normal speech is in the high-frequency range. Once those hair cells become damaged, it is difficult to understand speech, especially if the conversation takes place in a noisy club or at a party. What can be just another night of ear-pounding music to your friend can mean permanent hearing loss for you, simply because you and your friend are physically different.

So what's a musician to do? Plenty. First, use common sense when setting volume levels for both mains and monitors. If it seems too loud, it is. Ringing in the ears is the classic symptom of too-long exposure to loud sound. Even if you don't have ringing, you still may have sustained inner ear damage.

Many musicians wear ear plugs on stage to cut down the level of stimulation to the inner ear. You can buy the cheap foam or wax kinds at any drugstore; they work as well as the more expensive brands. If you feel you can't hear the music well enough with two ear plugs, try just one, preferably in the ear closest to the drummer. Always use the plug in the same ear. Drummers are especially at risk for hearing loss, so two plugs are recommended for them. Many rockers succumb to the vicious cycle of having to increase the volume because they have sustained hearing loss. The more they turn up, the more damage they inflict on their already fried inner ears.

If you are really serious about protecting your hearing, buy custom-made musician's ear plugs. These plugs are fitted by an audiologist and have a special filter that lets in sound while protecting the inner ear from damaging noise levels. As you can guess, these plugs are expensive. The wax or foam kinds of plug are effective and cheap. And if you lose them, you haven't lost an expensive piece of equipment.

On the Road

drug and alcohol problems, AIDS, and hearing loss are among the major dangers to be aware of in the music world. There are, however, other pitfalls that await the unsuspecting musician. Most gigs are at night, ending up with the band loading equipment at two in the morning. That means you'll be on the road just after the bars close. All those people who had a few too many will be out on the road, too. Be aware that late night is the most hazardous time for driving. Darkness decreases visibility, most people are tired, and more than a few are drunk. If you are playing a gig that is a distance from home, someone should stay up with the driver to keep him or her awake. Know when you need to switch drivers. It only takes a few seconds of falling asleep at the wheel to make a fatal accident.

Equipment Perils

You might think an aching back is your dad's problem, not yours. In reality, your father's back problems proabably started when he lifted things incorrectly as a young man. Speakers and power amps are your back's enemies. Here is the correct way to lift a large heavy object:

- Get a firm footing, with feet apart, toes pointed out.
- Bend at the knees, not at the waist. Maintain the natural curve in your back.
- Tighten stomach muscles that support your spine when you lift.
- Lift with your stronger leg muscles instead of your weaker back muscles.
- Keep the speaker or amp close to your body, if you are doing a single lift.
- Keep your back upright. Never twist your body when lifting or setting down.

When dealing with speakers or amps, two people sharing the burden is the way to go. Or invest in a dolly when you can't park close to your equipment's destination. Before you start unloading, clear the pathway of any potential dangers like spilled water, a slippery rug, or junk on the floor. When you are young, it is easy to think your body is indestructible. It isn't. Start good lifting habits now so you won't end up like Dad with his nagging backache.

The most important P.A. safety rule is: At an outdoor gig, stop playing and cover your equipment at the first drop of rain. Wet equipment acts as a conductor of electricity, channeling the electrical signal into your body when the mike or equipment is touched. Some shocks are just wake-up calls, others are blasts that create out-of-body experiences. Musicians have been electrocuted by their sound systems. It doesn't happen often, thank the music gods, but the potential is there when you mix liquid and electricity. Know enough not to play in the rain. If someone spills a drink on stage, wipe it up immediately. Electricity is the wonderful thing that makes your instrument or voice sound like it could fill the Grand Canyon. It can also fry you if you don't respect it.

To avoid shocks on stage, make sure your equipment and instruments are properly grounded. When your equipment is grounded, the extra electricity in the system goes into the ground instead of back into you as shocks from a mike or instrument. The third prong on an electrical plug is the grounding prong. Don't negate that prong by using a two-prong adapter. Most instrument amps have a ground lift button. Use this button when it is the only way to get rid of a terrible buzz. The safety features for grounding equipment are there to protect you. Don't defeat them.

The Breakup Blues

While you will hopefully survive the rigors of the music world intact, you must be prepared for the possibility that your band may not. Most bands either break up or lose or fire personnel at some time. Like a marriage, it is hard to know when to ride out the rough spots or file for divorce. Bands break up for a variety of reasons, most of which come under the heading of personality conflicts. But the biggest personality conflicts relate to differing opinions on musical direction.

Most new bands go through a honeymoon period during which the band works well together and has fun. But people grow in their music, and oftentimes that means their musical tastes change. Problems arise when band members don't agree on the musical direction that once carried them through good times and bad. Maybe the keyboard player wants to do more of his or her original material while the drummer wants to stick with the winning, though after a few years somewhat less exciting, cover format. Or maybe the rhythm guitar player is discovering the intricacies of jazz and wants to try more complex chord changes that throw the bass player for a loop.

Whatever the reason, change over time is part of maturing with your music. If a bandmate wants to explore new musical directions, try to keep an open mind about that person's ideas. True, the nature of the band may change. If, in your opinion, the change would be for the worse, it might be time to go your separate ways. But if you enjoy playing music with these people, don't throw it all away because something different looms on the horizon. If you have come to trust your musical comrades, listen to what they have to say. They might have something that could open up a whole new world for the group.

Trace the history of any great band, and you'll see that most have gone through many different stages. Whether change is part of a band's overall evolution or a death knell is a decision only you can make by listening to your feelings. If you decide it is time to leave the band, think about establishing another group with more like-minded players. Starting at ground zero with a new band can be daunting. But it can also be a fresh start for you to put into practice the knowledge gained from experience.

But sometimes people just need a break from the routine of rehearsals, gigs, recording, touring, and generally trying to crawl up the ladder of success. Before you decide to leave a certain band, ask yourself if the thing you can't tolerate can be remedied with communication, compromise, and patience. If you honestly feel it can't, it is probably wise to part company.

If a player decides to move on, evaluate what the band will be like without that person. Any group is a combination of the unique talents of the individuals in that band. The paradox is that no one is replaceable and everyone is replaceable. No one is replaceable in the sense that no guitarist plays exactly like the guitarist in your band. No other musician has exactly his or her talent or experience. By the same token, everyone is replaceable. Although your guitar player (obviously) plays guitar, so do a lot of other people. They may do it in a different way or have different strengths to bring to the band. But there are plenty of players out there eager to fill that empty slot. Keep in mind, the band will change when even one new member is added. Let the new person bring his or her style to the band without expecting or demanding that the person play exactly like the former player.

Deciding to leave a band is traumatic even when you know it is for the best. And having to ask someone to leave the band is the pits for everyone involved.

Here are a few reasons why band members get the boot:

- repeatedly showing up late for gigs
- having a drug or alcohol problem that interferes with the ability to act like a normal human being
- playing badly because of never practicing the material
- becoming romantically involved with a band member, then breaking up, making collaboration impossible
- stealing gig money

The list could go on, but you get the picture. If you want to stay in a band, work hard to make yourself an integral part of that band. As mentioned before, even if you are a killer player, you'll be history if you are too much of a pain in the butt.

Sex and the Single Band

Number four on the above list deserves a closer look. Starting a romance with a band member is a potential band-slayer. Potential is the key word because it is certainly possible for a couple to be in a band successfully. Nothing kicks in your hormones more than playing music with someone you are attracted to; if that attraction leads to a relationship, the other people in the band don't want to see you either constantly stuck on each other like white on rice or replaying Ralph and Alice from "The Honeymooners." A pair in a band can create a power block that can make other band members uncomfortable. It can also create jealousy and tension that can snuff out a band. To the couple in a band, strive to keep your personal life just that.

Love is grand, but when it goes bad and the couple is part of a band, everyone suffers. Think about how you would feel playing in a band with your former flame. If you can't handle the nuclear winter of playing in a band with your ex, who gets custody of the band? (Well, I've been in the band longer. Well, I'm more important because I'm the lead singer.) It could get ugly fast. All these traumas and more could be yours for the meager price of falling in love with a bandmate.

Conclusion

Hit Me With Music

There are very few basketball players who make the NBA. Likewise there are very few musicians who get on MTV or become famous. So the conclusion I've come to is that you've got to love what you do. Everything else is just a bonus.
Nick Travis,
bass player for the rock band
The Vanguard (formerly with
the band Apaches of Paris)[1]

Rock hits you. The music makes an impact on your life. And that impact inspired you to form a band. But you might want to play for more than just your love of music. It's natural to want your band, or perhaps one of your songs, to become a hit.

Many bands dream of the elusive "big time," a record deal with a major label that will bring your band to a national audience. If that is your dream, keep honing your music and building a local audience until that A & R (Artists & Repertoire) representative from Mega Music Corporation catches your act and decides you are destined to be the Next Big Thing. If your band is one of the lucky ones that nail a recording contract, realize that what you've done up until now has just been a warm-up. The real work begins after you sign on the dotted line. Hitting the big time means making a long-term commitment to your management team, which consists of your business manager, personal manager, booking agent, and lawyer. These people pay their bills from what they earn from you as a band. So don't be surprised if that team considers you a commodity to be marketed instead of just a group of talented musicians. One of the most difficult things for a new band that has broken through to a national audience is to keep its creative head together in the wake of the sometimes overwhelming business considerations. Also, realize that the music gods who snatched your band from obscurity can throw you back like an undersized fish. Many new bands whose recording sales fail to live up to the expectations of numbers-crunching executives don't get a second chance to record.

Those musicians who want to learn more about the business part of the music business should read Donald S. Passman's *All You Need to Know About the Music Business* and Alan H. Siegel's *Breaking into the Music Business*. Both books provide in-depth, humorous, and realistic looks at the music business.

But it is fun to dream. Every band that packs arenas and sells platinum albums started out as a local band. But for every band that "makes it," there are thousands of groups that never rise above local fame. And in all honesty, capturing local fame can be a bear, too. If you have fun playing and get enough gigs to satisfy yourself and your fans and keep your band together through thick and thin, you've succeeded where many have not.

Some young people who play in bands during their high school years find it tempting to drop out of school in order to concentrate on music. Studying for a history test may seem irrelevant when all you can think about is that big gig on Saturday night. If you are living at home and smoke comes out of your parents' ears when you talk about dropping out, don't. It's tough to put in the effort on something you don't think is important. But a high school diploma is important. What you learn, especially in your English and math classes, will come in handy in the music business more than you know. If music is really a part of your life, it will be there for that full-time effort after you graduate.

The reality of being in a band for most musicians is that you practice, rehearse, and play, either locally or out-of-town. It's cool to be in a band; it is also work. Some gigs are a blast, some you would like to have a hypnotist erase from your memory forever. The fact that you can make money from playing music is still one of life's sweet mysteries. Why some bands succeed while others do not is another. One band can break every rule in the music industry handbook and still ride a bullet to the top, while another group does everything "right" and can't get arrested.

Most people who play in bands when they are young do other things as time goes on. Yet many folks continue to play, gray hair and crow's feet notwithstanding. The love of music doesn't fade with the passing of time. Playing music, whether on stage or in a living room, is still as much of a kick for a fifty year-old as it is for a twenty-year old (though granted those kicks might have subtle differences). Just ask the Rolling Stones, the Grateful Dead, or any band that is still making noise after almost thirty years. So settle back, enjoy, and pace yourself. You have a long way to go.

notes

Introduction
1. Bob Marley, "Trenchtown Rock." *Bob Marley and the Wailers Live*, Island Records, 1975.

Chapter One
1. The Who, "Join Together." *The Kids Are Alright*, MCA Records, 1978.

Chapter Two
1. Quoted in Mick Wall, *Guns 'n' Roses: The Most Dangerous Band in the World* (New York: Hyperion, 1991), p. 125.
2. Quoted in David Sheff, *The Playboy Interviews with John Lennon & Yoko Ono* (New York: Playboy Press, 1981), p. 117.

Chapter Three
1. David Dalton, *The Rolling Stones: The First Twenty-Five Years* (New York: Knopf, 1981), p. 51.

Chapter Four
1. K. J. Dougton, *Metallica Unbound* (New York: Warner Books, 1993), pp. 94–96.

Chapter Five
1. Quoted in Roman Kozak, *This Ain't No Disco: The Story of CBGB* (Winchester, MA: Faber and Faber, 1988), p. 18.
2. Quoted in Joe Kohut and John J. Kohut, *Rock Talk: The Great Rock and Roll Quote Book* (Winchester, MA: Faber and Faber, 1994), p. 93.
3. Ibid p. 78.

Chapter Six
1. Kohut and Kohut, p. 155.
2. Ibid.

Chapter Seven
1. Quoted in *Option*, July / August 1994, p. 79.
2. Kohut and Kohut, p. 90.

Conclusion
1. Interview with Apaches of Paris, Austin, TX, February 8, 1994.

index